SINAI

in the SANCTUARY

JON HUNTZINGER, PHD

SINAI
in the SANCTUARY

*A Mountain
Theology*

TKU ✝ PRESS

Sinai in the Sanctuary: A Mountain Theology
Copyright 2017 © by Jon Huntzinger

Published jointly with Gateway Academic and TKU Press

ISBN: 978-1-945529-38-2 Paperback
ISBN: 978-1-945529-44-3 eBook
First Edition printed 2017

Gateway Academic, an imprint of Gateway Publishing exists to advance the Kingdom of God by
providing biblically and theologically sound resources to the Church and the Academy. We affirm the
Spirit-empowered calling of vocation and lay ministers and seek to create materials that shape
the mind and form the spirit.

We hope you hear from the Holy Spirit and receive God's richest blessings from this book by Gateway
Academic. We want to provide the highest quality resources that take the messages, music, and media
of Gateway Church to the world. For more information on other resources from Gateway Publishing,
go to gatewaypublishing.com.

Gateway Academic, an imprint of Gateway Publishing
700 Blessed Way
Southlake, Texas 76092
gatewaypublishing.com

Dedicated to Dr. Jack Hayford

Table of Contents

Foreword

FEW THINGS IN life are as fulfilling as the joy of watching a dear friend become truly accomplished in his chosen profession. Companion to this joy is the added delight when that profession is pursued with a clear-headed sense of "a call" to one's life-work—a call born of a faith in God void of superstition or fanaticism. The pleasure is even further amplified when this friend whom I consider a family member rises to a place of achievement that brings ever-increasing respect and commendation, both from seasoned observers as well as peers in his field. These are the reasons I feel such a profound delight in accepting Jon Huntzinger's invitation to provide the foreword for *Sinai in the Sanctuary*.

Convinced as I am that a book not only reveals the true character of the author, but also rises or falls in its potential influence proportionate to the *motivating spirit* of the author (i.e., not only his professional skill), I take double-delight in the work you have in hand. Both the man and the message herein are equally worthy of your time, thought, and practical application. *Sinai in the Sanctuary* ascends the mountain of God's glory, where His voice shakes the earth in fire and thunder, whispers and wind, and beckons believers to draw near. Though the climb bears the high cost of emptying oneself, the reward is the fulfillment of our true purpose—knowing God and being known by Him in His presence.

To be in any way informed, influenced, or simply acquainted with Jon Huntzinger is to be blessed by an encounter with "the real deal": a solid brother in Christ, a faithful husband and father, a serious and insightful scholar, and an infectious communicator. I am pleased to introduce this written work of his and hold the hope of more to come. I am persuaded that Jon's published appearance here is but the beginning of what will become an ever-increasing resource and fountain of refreshing and learning for leaders and learners in the Body of Christ.

Jack W. Hayford
Pastor Emeritus of The Church On The Way,
Van Nuys, California
Founder of The King's University,
Dallas, Texas

Introduction

MT. EVEREST IS the highest mountain in the world, rising 29,028 feet into the troposphere. The mystique and formidable majesty of the mountain yearly draw hundreds of climbers and adventurists who pay as much as $80,000 to climb its icy summit. Not everyone who attempts the climb survives, and some who do lose fingers, toes, and noses to frostbite in the effort. Yet, despite the high cost of the adventure and the very real risk to personal life, people from around the globe make their way to the border of Nepal and Tibet to follow in the steps of George Mallory who, when asked, "Why? Why did he climb the mountain?" answered with characteristic bravado, "Because it is there."

One mountain, however, figuratively ascends far higher than Everest. The Bible calls it Sinai or Mt. Horeb. Today, most people identify it with one of two peaks in the Sinai Peninsula—either Jebel Musa at 7,362 feet or Ras es-Safsafeh at 1,993 feet. Others believe Mt. Sinai is Jebel al-Lawz in the Arabian Peninsula, what once was ancient Midian. Though certainly not higher than Mt. Everest in terms of feet, it reaches up far higher in terms of significance and meaning. It extends up into the rarefied air where God speaks His word and makes known His will. It stretches up to where God's glory blazes in fire and His wisdom rumbles in thunder. It is a mountain that demands from those who dare climb its heights every bit as much commitment and sacrifice as that required of the men and women who scale Everest. That is because the men and women who climb Sinai must give more than time, money, and training to the endeavor—they must give all of their hearts, souls, and minds to the will of God made known there.

The reward for risking the summit of Everest, according to those who have managed the extraordinary feat, is the knowledge of rare accomplishment and an infusion of inspiration for living. Most who have stood at the apex of the earth talk about the life-changing nature of their climb. They say that from the moment they climbed the mountain, it became the measurement for the rest of their lives—a new standard for how they viewed the world and their place in it. So, too, the reward for risking Mt. Sinai is a complete and life-altering transformation. A new standard for living is found on Sinai, for it is there that one's true identity and purpose in life is discovered. At the pinnacle of Sinai, men and women discover that they are called to worship the Creator of the mountain and the One who gives them life. The reward of Sinai is the reward of worship. It is the reward of being known by God in His presence and exercising wise and discerning authority at the summit of His creation.[1]

---

1. Pastor Jack Hayford observes, "We are summoned to worship with such a dimensional reverence and sensitivity to His glorious presence and power that a new dimension of responsiveness transforms us." Hayford,

This study explores Scripture's stories of Mt. Sinai and follows the theological thread that flows from the mountain. Sinai's theology is one of revelation, vocation, and mission: revelation of understanding found in the word God speaks to His people; vocation in the worship of God who speaks His word; and mission to lead the world in the worship of God through the revelation of that word.

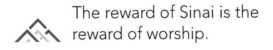 The reward of Sinai is the reward of worship.

This study is also an example of *internarrativity*. Internarrativity describes the presence and influence of earlier biblical stories in later ones. Much like *intertextuality*, which studies the presence of earlier biblical texts in those that come later by means of quotations or allusions, internarrativity discerns the presence of foundational biblical stories in those that were written later.[2] Stories featuring Adam and the garden, Abraham and faith, Moses and deliverance, and David and the kingdom continued to resonate with the people of Israel throughout the centuries. They were remembered by later generations and

---

The Reward of Worship, 13. The empowerment that attends such transformation in worship results in greater power and authority in life. He writes, "Worship, in a very real sense of the word, opens a doorway to the power of His presence." Ibid., 27.

2. Internarrativity differs from what scholars call tradition criticism in that it emphasizes story connections in addition to thematic ones. Since story involves character and plot as well as theme, an internarrative reading of biblical texts looks for similarities in what is revealed about the characters and how the plot of the story is developed while tracing the theme of the story.

impacted how those people understood their present-day circumstances. The biblical writers and those who heard their prophecies, sang their songs, studied their laws, and puzzled over their apocalyptic visions, did so through the prism of the stories of their ancestors. The very air they breathed in their homes, villages, and synagogues was filled with these identity-shaping stories.

Not only did the people of Israel breathe in the air of these stories, but they also lived them year in and year out. In particular, the Exodus was the definitive story by which they viewed themselves. Each year, the people relived the deliverance of their fathers and mothers from slavery in Egypt when they gathered in Jerusalem to celebrate Passover, later Pentecost, and finally Tabernacles. That foundational story wasn't consigned to the distant past but renewed annually and remained a present reality to the people. They didn't just remember the Exodus each year; they lived it out when they ate bitter herbs at Passover, waved sheaves of barley at Pentecost, and built small dwellings at Tabernacles. They joined themselves to their ancestors in this way and, in so doing, wove a thread of memory that connected their present to their past. Through this living memory, the people preserved the faith of their fathers and continued to experience it in their own lives.

By telling and living out the old stories of the Bible, the people linked their present life and circumstances with that of their ancestors to give it perspective. They heard, recited, studied, memorized, and remembered those stories preserved by the biblical writers who were convinced that they were living out God's eternal covenantal purposes in the present and so drew from the lives of Adam, Abraham, and Moses to interpret their own circumstances. The Apostle Paul reveals this mindset when he recalls the story of the Exodus for the Corinthians: "These things took place as examples for us" (1 Corinthians 10:6). In Paul's mind, the inaugural story of deliverance provided a prophetic perspective on the Gentile Corinthians' own story and situation. To the Romans, Paul says, "For whatever was written in former days was written for our instruction, that through endurance and through the encouragement of the Scriptures we might have hope" (Romans 15:4). That Paul drew on the ancient Scriptures and the stories they preserved to give meaning to present circumstances has long been observed and discussed.[3] Even so, it is important to remind ourselves how profoundly men like Paul were shaped by those formative stories and how illustrative they were for them.[4]

The retelling of the Exodus is found throughout the Old and New Testaments. It became the primary narrative by which the people of Israel viewed their banishment in Exile hundreds of years later, and it was the source for numerous songs sung at the temple (Psalms 68, 77, 78, 106). It influenced the evangelists as they composed their

---

3. For example, see Hays, *The Conversion of the Imagination.*
4. Wenham, *Story as Torah.* Old Testament scholar Gordon Wenham says those earliest stories shaped the behavior and way of living of later biblical communities.

Gospels, Paul and Peter as they wrote their epistles, the preacher of Hebrews, and the visionary John.

At the center of the Exodus story towers Mt. Sinai. It is there God gives His commandments to Israel and makes a covenant with them. It is there He lays out the plans for the tabernacle and establishes the way of worship for His people. And it is there He calls the people to sonship in relationship with Him and to His priesthood, with the high privilege of leading the nations in His service. Sinai is the place where God is present in glory to reveal His word, call His people to worship in freedom, and establish the way that they are to bring transformation to the world. Sinai is the place where God's wisdom and authority is revealed in purifying power for people of faith.

1

Sonship and Worship

THE STORY OF the Exodus is one of deliverance for worship.
It is a story that describes the formation of a people for the
specific privilege of worshipping God. The people chosen
for this privilege are not free, rich, or powerful; rather, they
are enslaved, poor, and weak. They don't live in their own
land. They don't worship in their own temple. They don't
even remember the name of their God. Yet, God chooses
such a people to hear His word and live in relationship with
Him. He chooses them to become a new priesthood of sons
and daughters who will lead the world in worship.

This calling begins when God appears to Moses in fire
on a mountain in the wilderness of Midian and promises to
lead the Israelites out of slavery into freedom and blessing.
God says He will give them a land of abundance:

> "I have come down to deliver them out of the hand of
> the Egyptians and to bring them up out of that land
> to a good and broad land, a land flowing with milk
> and honey" (Exodus 3:8).

This land is not like Egypt where the people have lived in
bondage and ignorance. It is a land of freedom and wisdom

where they will live by the light of God's word. Moses exhorts the Israelites to keep the commandments because they represent God's wisdom to them:

> Keep and do them for that will be your wisdom and your understanding in the sight of the peoples, who, when they hear all these statutes, will say, "Surely this great nation is a wise and understanding people" (Deuteronomy 4:6).

There in the wilderness, God tells Moses that Mt. Sinai will be a sign of calling and purpose:

> "I will be with you and this shall be the sign for you that I have sent you: when you have brought the people out of Egypt, you shall serve God on this mountain" (Exodus 3:12).

The Hebrew word for *serve* here is *avad* which means *worship*. The worship the people offer God at that mountain will signify that His word to Moses is true and He is faithful and able to do all that He says. There at the mountain, the people will gather and worship God as they receive His commandments. Worship will be the sign of their deliverance, and Mt. Sinai a symbol of worship, both made possible by the freedom-giving power of God through His word.

Worship will be the sign of their deliverance, and Mt. Sinai a symbol of worship, both made possible by the freedom-giving power of God through His word.

MULTICULTURAL MOSES

Who is this man God calls to lead the people into freedom
for worship? To whom does God speak out of fire? Old
Testament scholar George Coats calls Moses a liberator,
shepherd, and lawgiver. He says that Moses is both a heroic
man who leads the people in authority as well as a man of
God who follows Him in obedience.[1] In addition to being
a hero and man of God, Scripture shows Moses to be a
man of three cultures who speaks the languages of three
peoples. He is a Hebrew, an Egyptian, and a Midianite
and thus speaks of deliverance and worship in ways each
of those nations can understand. Moses is Hebrew by
birth to Levitical parents, Egyptian through adoption
into Pharaoh's family, and Midianite in marriage to the
daughter of Jethro the priest. As a son of slaves, an adopted
grandson of a king, and a son-in-law of a national priest,
he experiences obedience (Hebrew), authority (Egyptian),
and devotion (Midianite) throughout his life. The trajec-
tory of Moses' life thus moves from obedience to authority
and from authority to worship.

As a Hebrew, Moses feels the suffering of the Israelites
who are being beaten down by their Egyptian masters. He
identifies with them in their anguish:

> One day ... [Moses] saw an Egyptian beating a
> Hebrew, one of his people. He looked this way and
> that, and seeing no one, he struck down the Egyptian
> and hid him in the sand (Exodus 2:11–12).

---

1. Coats, *Moses: Heroic Man, Man of God*, 157–166.

Moses sees the burden his familial people carry and acts on their behalf. He is affected by the condition of the people of his ancestry and birth. In addition to this, as an Egyptian, Moses possesses knowledge of the culture and religion of a great dynastic people. He knows their history, their ways, and the gods they serve. Even more, he knows the procedures of the palace and the practices followed there. He knows who to talk to and what steps to take to gain access to Pharaoh. Finally, as a Midianite, Moses appreciates the tribal ways of those who live on the semiarid plateaus far to the east of Egypt. He knows their family life and the customs they follow. He understands tribal hierarchy and the importance of honor among a proud people.

All of this means that Moses speaks of worship with knowledge and understanding in the tongues of three diverse peoples. To the Hebrews, he speaks the promise of worship: "I will be with you, and ... when you have brought the people out of Egypt, you shall [worship me] on this mountain" (Exodus 3:12). To the Egyptians, he speaks the command of worship: "Let God's people go to worship" (Exodus 4:23). And to the Midianites, he speaks the welcome of worship by allowing his father-in-law to offer sacrifices to God because, as Jethro says, "I know that the Lord is greater than all gods." (Exodus 18:11). Altogether, Moses speaks the promise of worship to Israel, issues the command of worship to Pharaoh, and facilitates the beginning of worship among the nations with the Midianites.

Moses speaks to these peoples on behalf of the God of Abraham, Isaac, and Jacob. God has seen the affliction of the Israelites and promises to deliver them and give them a new land (Exodus 3:17). He says that He will give a sign to Moses that He has sent him to the people. As already noted, this sign is the freedom to worship at Mt. Sinai and will confirm the purpose of their deliverance. It will attest to the faithful power of God to deliver and answer any doubts that may linger in their minds. Is the deliverance a matter of Moses' own natural talents? Is it a matter of good fortune or the convergence of natural events? Is it a matter of Pharaoh's mismanagement and poor leadership? The worship at Mt. Sinai will confirm the purpose of their deliverance and show that it is not the result of Moses' ability, Pharaoh's inability, or natural calamity, but rather of God's love and charity (Deuteronomy 7:7–8). God performs the signs in the deliverance, like the parting of the sea and the gift of manna, so the people will know what He is doing in their midst. The most important of these is the sign of worship at Mt. Sinai.

> God performs the signs in the deliverance, like the parting of the sea and the gift of manna, so the people will know what He is doing in their midst. The most important of these is the sign of worship at Mt. Sinai.

SONSHIP AND WORSHIP AT SINAI

This worship is inextricably connected to God's word. Specifically, it is linked to the ten words He speaks at Sinai, which we know as the Ten Commandments. Along with these words, God gives Moses many others having to do with Israel's life together with Him. Much of the Book of Exodus and all the Book of Leviticus outline the way of worship between the people and God. In Exodus, the Ten Commandments are followed by instructions for the tabernacle and its furnishings, sacrificial offerings, priests and their garments, and the Sabbath. Leviticus gives detailed instructions on offerings, purity, priests, feasts, and social life. Taken together, these two books describe the way of worship for a people of worship. And all of this is given to Moses by God at Mt. Sinai.[2]

The importance of this worship for Israel can be heard in the message that God gives Moses to deliver to Pharaoh—"Let my people go!" This message, so dramatically intoned by Charlton Heston in Cecil B. DeMille's movie *The Ten Commandments*, is not only about worship but also about sonship:

> Then you shall say to Pharaoh, "Thus says the LORD, Israel is my firstborn son, and I say to you, 'Let my son go that he may serve [worship] me.' If you refuse to let him go, behold, I will kill your firstborn son" (Exodus 4:22–23, emphasis added).

The purpose of the deliverance is neither for Israel merely to experience relief from her heavy burdens, nor to eat fig cakes and enjoy a life of ease. It is for God's son to escape bondage in Egypt, freely worship his Father on the mountain, and thereby discover who he was created to be.

---

2. For more on tabernacle worship, see Hayford, *The Reward of Worship*, 183–195.

This means that the worship Israel will offer to God will be given both in freedom and in relationship. The people will not worship God as an enslaved nation but as an embraced son. It is not the worship of compulsion that Israel will give but one of devotion. It is the devotion of a son to a loving Father. It will take time for this revelation to transform the Israelites' understanding of God and themselves, but the story of the deliverance begins by describing worship in the familial context of father and son. It begins on Mt. Sinai.

WARFARE OVER SONSHIP AND WORSHIP

That this deliverance for sonship and worship amounts to warfare is highlighted by the fact that Moses goes to Pharaoh seven times to demand the release of the Hebrew people so that they may go into the wilderness to serve God (Exodus 5:1; 7:16; 8:1, 20; 9:1, 13; 10:3). Stubbornly, Pharaoh refuses Moses' demand. Given that "pharaoh was always the focal point of Egyptian religion, the ultimate high priest who built temples and oversaw their maintenance,"[3] his refusal represents a religious and spiritual resistance to the worship of Moses' God. This spiritual struggle begins with the defilement of the Nile River and continues through the plagues of frogs, gnats, flies, death of livestock, boils, hail, and locusts, until Pharaoh's advisors say to him, "How long shall this man be a snare to us? Let the men go, that

---

3. Hoffmeier, "Egyptians," 283.

they may [worship] the Lord their God. Do you not yet understand that Egypt is ruined?" (Exodus 10:7). "In Egyptian thought, the king was responsible for the proper functioning of the Nile, agricultural fertility, and even the sun's rising. The plagues show that Moses' God is 'responsible for maintaining cosmic order' and ultimately deserving of worship, not Pharaoh."[4]

Even though his nation and land is descending into chaos due to his refusal to let the Hebrew people worship God, Pharaoh doesn't perceive that the plagues represent creation's rebellion against his intransigence, or stubbornness. He doesn't understand that *creation itself is crying out for the sons and daughters of God to be released for worship*. The land longs for the revelation of their sonship. It yearns to see these sons and daughters be the image of their Father and reflect His likeness in their worship as He originally intended. It aches to be released from its own bondage caused by Adam's disobedience not long after creation. In short, the land of Egypt wants the Israelites— the sons of God (Exodus 4:22)—to go and worship, and it is in agony over Pharaoh's refusal. These events preview the Apostle Paul's insight that all creation awaits the revelation of the sons and daughters of God and eagerly anticipates their worship of Him (Romans 8:19). The plagues of Egypt represent the groans and uprising of the land against Pharaoh's antagonistic, anti-worship attitude.

Thus, as darkness descends over the land, Pharaoh finally tells Moses to worship but to leave the children and

---

4. Ibid., 288.

animals behind. Moses will not compromise and says the children must participate and the animals must be part of the worship as sacrifices. Pharaoh refuses one last time and orders Moses away from his presence (Exodus 10:21–29).[5] The deepening darkness is a final sign of the king's devolving attitude toward worship despite all the other signs God has given him.

SINAI THEOLOGY

God delivers Israel from bondage in Egypt so the people might enter into a worshipful relationship with Him as sons and daughters. It is there at Sinai that God makes Himself known by speaking His words to them and showing them in those words how they are to worship as sons and daughters. The desert mountain is a symbol of God's self-revelation through His word and His desire to have a relationship with Israel who will worship Him.

The fact that God orders Pharaoh to release Israel to worship Him seven times underscores the meaning of their deliverance. It bears repeating: freedom to worship as sons and daughters of God is the sign of a delivered people.

It bears repeating: freedom to worship as sons and daughters of God is the sign of a delivered people.

5. Throughout chapter 10, the verb *serve* originates *avad* and means *worship*.

God's revelation to Israel at Sinai is ultimately for all people. He wants us to experience deliverance in our lives and to know Him. He wants us to enter into a worshipful relationship with Him. He desires to deliver each of us from our places of bondage so that we may freely worship in His presence as sons and daughters. Such worship is a sign of Sinai in our midst.

Reflection and Discussion

1. Why did God deliver the Israelites from bondage in Egypt?
2. What do the plagues that afflict Egypt represent other than God's judgment?
3. What connection do you see between your worship of God and His saving grace in your life?

2

The Fiery Bush

IT WAS WHILE Moses was leading the flock of his father-in-law Jethro, a Midianite priest, into the wilderness that he initially made his way to "the mountain of God." For the first time, though not the last, Moses saw fire on the mountain. There he saw a small tree engulfed in flames but neither burned nor charred (Exodus 3:1–3).

A PURIFIED PEOPLE

That God speaks from the midst of a small burning tree is prophetic, revealing His intention to live within Israel as holy fire. He will not be present to His people as destructive fire, to judge or condemn them for their impurity, but rather as tempering fire to consecrate Israel for worship. God knows the people He intends to deliver. He understands that they have lived in Egypt for hundreds of years and have become acculturated to Egyptian ways of thinking and living. The people have learned Egyptian religion and become familiar with Egyptian gods.[1] They

---

1. This Egyptian influence is evident when the people, thinking that Moses has died on the mountain in the midst of the fire, fashion an idol

have sung their songs and listened to their wise men. The Israelites have been so influenced by their life in Egypt that they have, for all practical understanding, become Egyptian. As such, they have become impure and unable to offer the kind of worship God desires.

The sign of the fiery bush means that God will be present with the people to purify them for worship. In the Old Testament, Israel is at times depicted as a tree.[2] Here, the people are described as a "thorny bush" or small tree (*sĕneh*) because they are few and will be difficult to reach, like a rose bush that requires careful handling because of its thorns. God did not choose this people because of their robust faith or good nature. In fact, the Old Testament described them as rebellious; they show themselves to be difficult and slow to believe throughout their years of wandering. According to the psalmist, the people are

> A stubborn and rebellious generation,
> a generation whose heart was not steadfast,
> whose spirit was not faithful to God
> (Psalm 78:8).

The sign of the fiery bush means that God will be present with the people to purify them for worship.

---

in the form of a golden calf. The idol may have been of the god Ptah, who was represented in the form of a calf.

2. See Nielsen, *There Is Hope for a Tree*, for her discussion of how the metaphor of a tree is used to refer to Israel in Isaiah.

Time after time, the people grumble about their situation and accuse Moses of leading them out of Egypt to see them die in the desert (Exodus 5:21; 14:10–12; 16:1–8; 17:1–7; 32:1–6; Numbers 11–14). Nonetheless, God shows His love and great power by delivering a small, poor, difficult, and disbelieving people from slavery. The fiery bush is a sign of God's presence among such men and women (few, impoverished, and prickly though they may be) to burn away their impurities so that they can worship Him.[3]

NAMES AND SIGNS AT SINAI

When Moses draws near to the fiery bush, God speaks three words and reveals His plans for His people. First, the Lord says that He knows their suffering: "I have surely seen the affliction of my people who are in Egypt and have heard their cry because of their taskmasters. I know their sufferings" (Exodus 3:7). God doesn't merely understand their suffering in a detached, intellectual way; rather, He has shared in it and has been impacted by it somehow. Furthermore, God hasn't heard the sound from His people that He desires. He wants to hear their joy and gladness, their praises, but all He hears is their cry of suffering and groaning. Instead of worship, His ears are filled with wailing.[4]

---

3. The Book of Leviticus emphasizes the importance of purity as God commands the people to be holy as He is holy.
4. The Old Testament rarely uses the word for *groaning* (ne'āqāh). It describes the cries of Israel during the time of the judges when they were oppressed by surrounding nations (Judges 2:18). It also refers to

The people of Israel groaned because of their
slavery and cried out for help. Their cry for rescue
from slavery came up to God. And God heard their
groaning, and God remembered his covenant with
Abraham, with Isaac, and with Jacob. God saw the
people of Israel—and God knew (Exodus 2:23–25).

Second, God pledges to lead the people to a rich land: "I
promise that I will bring you up out of the affliction of
Egypt to the land ... flowing with milk and honey"
(Exodus 3:17). This promise relates to His purpose for the
people to worship Him: "Go to the king of Egypt and say to
him, 'The Lord, the God of the Hebrews, has met with us;
and now, please let us go a three days' journey into the
wilderness, that we may sacrifice to the Lord our God'"
(Exodus 3:18). Not only does God know their desperate
existence, but He also knows what they need to live freely
in a worshipful relationship with Him, and He is
committed to providing it for them.

> Not only does God know
> their desperate existence,
> but He also knows what they need
> to live freely in a worshipful relation-
> ship with Him, and He is committed
> to providing it for them.

Finally, God gives His name to Moses and the Israelites:
"I am who I am." *I am* is the eternal name of the God

---

the cries of Egypt when that nation was judged by God at the time of the
Exile (Ezekiel 30:24).

of Abraham, Isaac, and Jacob (Exodus 3:13–15). God's message to Moses and the Israelites is that He knows His family. He knows their condition, promises to deliver them from it, and *gives His name as a pledge that He will fulfill His promise*. Later, the Lord elaborates on His name when Moses returns to Mt. Sinai and asks to see His glory. God says of Himself, "The Lord, the Lord, a God merciful and gracious, slow to anger, and abounding in steadfast love and faithfulness, keeping steadfast love for thousands, forgiving iniquity and transgression and sin, but who will by no means clear the guilty." (Exodus 34:6–7). Moses bows to the ground in response, worships the Lord, and asks, "Let the Lord go in the midst of us, ... and take us for your inheritance" (Exodus 34:9).

Later rabbis read this passage and discerned as many as thirteen attributes or names for God in it. Just a casual glance reveals that the God to whom Moses bows is merciful, gracious, patient, loving, forgiving, and righteous. He intends to dwell among His sons and daughters. These attributes constitute the names that God possesses in His relationship with Moses and the people.[5] They are the names by which He will be worshipped, and they are revealed on Mt. Sinai. God makes Himself known on the mountain so His people can worship Him with understanding. At the same time, He wants them to know they are the sons and daughters of *I Am* because it is only with such knowledge that they can truly worship Him.

---

5. See Knowles, *The Unfolding Mystery,* for an elaboration on the attributes or names of God listed in Exodus 34.

As God reveals His names on the mountain in fire, He invests Moses with the authority to deliver the people. God pledges that He will perform miracles by which they will know what He is doing in their midst. Thus, the first miracle is that of Moses' rod. It becomes a snake when thrown to the ground and returns to its original form when picked up (Exodus 4:1–5). This miracle signifies God's authority over the deity powers of Egypt in that the snake was an amulet of an Egyptian god affixed to Pharaoh's crown. The power to pick up the snake demonstrates Moses' God-given authority over Pharaoh and the demonic powers of Egypt.[6]

Moses' diseased hand is the second miracle (Exodus 4:6–7). His hand turns leprous when he places it inside his cloak and removes it, and it becomes clean when he puts it back and then takes it out again. Leprosy was viewed as something more than a chronic skin condition in the ancient world.[7] It was symbolic of a person's spiritual condition. This sign reveals that God's intention, in the deliverance of Israel from slavery, is to cleanse His people of their impurity. His goal is to make them pure so they can enjoy a relationship with Him. The rottenness of the disease represents the spiritual condition of the people

---

6. George Coats observes that the rod is symbolic of obedience as well as power: "It stands for the authority Moses carries for commanding obedience." Coats, 67. Later he writes, "Moses the hero acts by the power of God, a unique union symbolized by the Mosaic rod." (Ibid., 165).

7. *Eerdman's Dictionary of the Bible, 801.* The word *leprosy* translates the Hebrew ṣaraʿaṯ, which likely describes various types of skin conditions but not Hansen's disease that destroys the skin, membrane, and nerves of a body.

who have become unclean as a result of their years of servitude in Egypt. Like lepers everywhere at that time who were prohibited from living in the midst of their own people, the people of Israel have been living outside the country God promised to their father Abraham (Genesis 12:7, 15:7–21, 17:8). But God intends to make them clean and return them to their homeland where they can worship Him in righteousness, just as Abraham did.[8]

The third miracle is the turning of Nile River water into blood when poured onto dry ground. This unusual sign demonstrates what will happen when Pharaoh refuses to release the Israelites to worship. It shows what will befall the Egyptians in the beginning when the river turns to blood, and it also foreshadows the destruction of the Egyptians in the waters of the Red Sea at the end. As they race over dry ground in pursuit of the Israelites, the sea will surge over them and drown them. The first and last signs of God's deliverance given in the waters of the Nile River and the Red Sea are one and the same: water becomes blood.

THE VIOLENCE OF SINAI

These miracles show that the purification of God's people for worship may involve force, which is neither indiscriminate nor punitive. Rather, it is measured, restorative, and represents a controlled response to the

---

8. Israel's righteous worship will be given as they faithfully live by the commandments of the covenant that God makes with them.

force used to enslave the Hebrew people and the resistance thrown up against God's desire for worship. Such violence reflects what Hans Boersma in his discussion of God's election and deliverance of Israel describes as His "preferential hospitality" for His people.[9] God comes to the defense of a small, poor, and ignorant people in "preferential hospitality" at the same time He acts against the powerful and wealthy Egyptians in a "violence of reprobation."[10] Such action opens the way to a land of abundance so that the Hebrews may worship Him. This is only the beginning, however. God's violence is not limited to Israel's favor; rather, it is intended to benefit all people. "The purpose of divine hospitality is ultimately not just to draw Israel into a relationship with God, but also to restore the intimacy of love with all humanity and with the entire created order."[11]

The fire of Sinai is symbolic of violence that results in hospitality of relationship. It is not destructive (the tree is not burned up) but rather brings about purification through God's presence among His people. It reveals God to be a Refiner who will remove the dross and impurity of Egypt from the Hebrews so they may show His glory with perfect translucence as sons and daughters. The fiery bush shows that God's hospitality is deliverance from slavery for the purpose of purely reflecting God's glory in worship.

---

9. Boersma, *Violence, Hospitality, and the Cross*, 79–88.
10. Ibid., 75–88.
11. Ibid., 87.

SINAI'S PURIFICATION IN MALACHI

The fire of this first story of Sinai in Scripture points ahead to the last story of the Old Testament. The violence and resulting hospitality represented in the fiery bush reappear in the Book of Malachi. There, the prophet reports God's contention with His people who have become indifferent in their worship before Him and constantly argue and quibble with Him about it. They disbelieve the words of His prophets in the same way the Israelites disbelieved the words of Moses. Why has this happened? Hasn't God brought them back to their land after the Babylonian Exile? Hasn't He kept His promises to them of a highway in the wilderness (Isaiah 40)? To the people's way of thinking, God has not. The great promises they had heard about the return to the land have not come to pass. Most disheartening is the temple. The people look upon it and see a shadow of its former brilliance (Haggai 2:3). They wonder what happened to the glorious temple that Ezekiel envisioned (Ezekiel 40–48). They express disappointment similar to the Israelites in the wilderness, who grew tired of eating God's manna and said,

> "Oh that we had meat to eat! We remember the fish we ate in Egypt that cost nothing, the cucumbers, the melons, the leeks, the onions, and the garlic. But now our strength is dried up, and there is nothing at all but this manna to look at" (Numbers 11:4–6).

In their disappointment, the people at the time of Malachi have become similarly lethargic in their worship and so dishonor God with their halfhearted offerings of blind, lame, and sick animals. Malachi voices God's despair:

> "O priests, who despise my name. But you say, 'How have we despised your name?' By offering polluted food upon my altar. But you say, 'How have we polluted you?' By saying that the Lord's table may be despised. When you offer blind animals in sacrifice, is that not evil? And when you offer those that are lame or sick, is that not evil? Present that to your governor; will he accept you or show you favor?" (Malachi 1:6–8).

The people despise the Lord's Table by offering animals they would have culled out of their herds anyway in the same way the Israelites despised the Lord's provision in the wilderness and longed for the days of servitude back in Egypt. Malachi's people give God their leftovers and hand-me-downs and expect Him to be satisfied, just as Moses' people yearned for the leftovers of Egypt. Yet, God wants to be present to the Jewish people of the 5th century BC, just as He was to their ancestors a thousand years earlier, and He intends to purify them as He did their fathers and mothers in the wilderness.

According to Malachi, God has seen enough and vows to appear to His people because of His love for them.[12] Though the people have ceased to worship truly

---

12. The fact that the book begins with the declaration "I have loved you, says the Lord" (Malachi 1:2) reveals that God's anger and grief over His people's lack of worship arises out of His love for them. It also explains His commitment to send His messenger to them to renew their ability to worship in person.

and their offerings are as unworthy as the priests are
profane, nonetheless God will come to them. Before He
does, however, He will send a messenger to prepare for
His coming, since no one can endure His appearance
otherwise. The messenger will make a way for the Lord,
who Himself will refine and purify the people. Just like He
did for the Hebrews coming out of Egypt through Moses,
so He will do for the Jews who have come out of exile: He
will purify them for worship.

> He is like a refiner's fire and like fullers' soap. He will
> sit as a refiner and purifier of silver, and he will purify
> the sons of Levi and refine them like gold and silver,
> and they will bring offerings in righteousness to the
> Lord (Malachi 3:2–3).

The coming of the Lord will be violent and involve
kiln-blasting refinement to bring about hospitality in the
form of new worship among the people. Sadly, not all will
experience hospitality. Malachi concludes with a description of a future day that will burn like an oven and "the
arrogant and all evildoers will be stubble. The day that is
coming shall set them ablaze" (Malachi 4:1). The prophet
envisions the coming of the Lord as refinement of His
people for worship, even as it judges the proud and those
who refuse to do so.

That Malachi sees the circumstances of his time similar
to those of the Hebrew people in Egypt is apparent in
his description of them as God's "treasured possession"
(Malachi 3:17), recalling the identity that God gave the
Israelites in the wilderness at Mt. Sinai (Exodus 19:5–6;

Deuteronomy 7:6, 26:18). It is also apparent in the final verses of his message, where he exhorts them to "remember the law of my servant Moses, the statutes and rules that I commanded him at Horeb (Sinai) for all Israel" (Malachi 4:4). He draws their attention back to the mountain where God was present to the people, gave them His law, and called them to worship. They are to remember the way of worship established by God's words at Sinai (in the commandments, plans for the tabernacle, and ritual worship) and thus experience its present blessing in their lives. Malachi prophesies that when they return to pure worship, God will throw open "the windows of heaven ... and pour down for [them] a blessing until there is no more need," and "all nations will call [them] blessed, for [they] will be a land of delight" (Malachi 3:10, 12). Pure worship results in the fulfillment of their divine vocation, which is to lead the nations in appreciation and adoration of God, who in the past led their ancestors out of Egypt. This worship results in riches and blessing, such as was given originally to Israel at Mt. Sinai.

SINAI THEOLOGY

The fiery bush on Sinai shows that God will be present with His people to purify them for worship. They will know Him by name as His sons and daughters and have all they need in a land of plenty to serve Him. This promise is too great for the people to believe without help, so God gives signs to strengthen their faith. The first shows that Moses possesses the authority to lead them out of Egypt. His power is greater than the powers of Pharaoh and Pharaoh's gods. The second shows the result of this deliverance. The people will be made pure to offer worship to God. The third sign shows the power by which God will deliver them when the Egyptians refuse to let them go.

The fire of Sinai shows that just as God was a deliverer to Moses and the Israelites and a refiner to Malachi and the people of Judah, so also is He a deliverer and refiner for us today. He acts with compassion and at times with irresistible force to create a pure people to worship Him. God has called us to the vocation of worship and personally works in our lives to carry out our high calling. This calling is not to worship God alone, however, but to lead the nations in such worship too.

The revelation of Sinai is that God helps those He loves to worship Him. Not only does He make himself known to us by giving us His name, but also He knows us as well. He knows our histories, our achievements and failures, and He works in us to enjoy relationship with Him. Where there is weakness, He gives us strength, and where there is impurity, He is present to purify us.

Reflection and Discussion

1. What is the meaning of the bush that is on fire but does not burn to ashes?
2. How is the message of the Book of Malachi like the message of the story of the deliverance of Israel?
3. What areas of your own life has God purified or is purifying? How hard has it been to be purified by God? What has been the result of God's loving, purifying work in you?

3

Moses at Sinai: A Kingdom of Priests

GOD'S TREASURE AND THE NATIONS' PRIESTHOOD

After Moses leads Israel through the Red Sea and into the wilderness, the people eventually make their way to Mt. Sinai. When they arrive, Moses goes up the mountain where he first heard God's promise.[1] This time, God specifies the purpose for Israel's deliverance: "You shall be my treasured possession among all peoples, for all the earth is mine; and you shall be to me a kingdom of priests and a holy nation" (Exodus 19:5–6). Here God names the people of Israel and establishes their identity as His possession. He knows their familial history as the children of Abraham, Isaac, and Jacob, and He knows their suffering in Egypt. In fact, the Hebrew word for *know* (*yadah*) in this passage indicates that God has shared in

---

1. Hort, "The Plagues of Egypt," 69 (1957), 84–103, and 70 (1958), 48–59. The return to Egypt, the period of the plagues, and the eventual exodus from the land would have slowly occurred over many months. Old Testament scholar Greta Hort shows how the plagues may have been interrelated and have had natural causes that evolved over a period of time.

Israel's suffering in some personal way (Exodus 2:23–24).
He has not looked upon their ordeal from afar with a
detached eye but has experienced it and has now brought
them to this place to tell them that they belong to Him as a
"treasured possession" and that they belong to the nations
as "a kingdom of priests." They will fulfill their dual role
both to God and the nations by being a "holy nation" in
possession of God's holy words. [2] They will be holy even as
their God is holy (Leviticus 11:45, 19:2, 20:26). All that
follows the Ten Commandments, including the festivals,
the building of the tabernacle, and the preparation of
Aaron and his sons to serve as priests, elaborates on
Israel's identity as God's treasure and the nations' priesthood. Israel will worship God and lead the world in godly
worship by living according to the words He gives to
Moses on the mountain.

> They will fulfill their dual
> role both to God and the
> nations by being a "holy nation" in
> possession of God's holy words.

The people prepare to receive God's words and learn the
way of worship by washing and waiting for His arrival.

On the morning of the third day there were thunders
and lightnings and a thick cloud on the mountain and
a very loud trumpet blast.... Now Mount Sinai was
wrapped in smoke because the Lord had descended

---

2. The exact translation of the Hebrew (*asreh dĕḇarîm*) is *ten words*.

on it in fire. The smoke of it went up like the smoke
of a kiln, and the whole mountain trembled greatly.
And as the sound of the trumpet grew louder and
louder, Moses spoke, and God answered him in
thunder (Exodus 19:16–19).

Thunder, lightning, smoke, and fire signify the volcanic
presence of God on the mountain. Whereas fire engulfed
a small tree the first time Moses climbed Mt. Sinai, this
time it engulfs the entire mountaintop. At Moses' first visit
to the mountain, God revealed who He was and what He
was about to do—I Am who would lead the people to a land
of milk and honey to worship Him. Now He reveals who
the people are (a priesthood) and what they will do (lead
others in worship).

FAITH AND FEAR AT SINAI

To enter the presence of a holy God and worship Him is
not for the faint of heart, but rather for the faithful of
heart. [3] It is for those who want what God wants, regardless of the requirements or personal consequences. Moses
was such a person. He was faithful of heart and wanted the
things God desired when he lived in Pharaoh's house. This
is evident in the story of his calling. God not only called
Moses because of his multicultural background (Hebrew,
Egyptian, and Midianite) but also because of his attitude.
When Moses used physical force to strike down an

---

3. The Hebrew word *lēb* signifies the volitional and decision-making
   center of a person's life.

Egyptian overseer who was beating a defenseless Hebrew worker, he showed his zeal for the defenseless. When he drove away shepherds who had taken over the springs from the daughters of Jethro, he showed his zeal for the weak a second time. God saw Moses' actions and chose him to deliver the people of Israel because He knew that Moses shared His concern for the weak and vulnerable.

> To enter the presence of a holy God and worship Him is not for the faint of heart, but rather for the faithful of heart.

Moses's faithful heart leads him up the mountain while the people remain below and withdraw in fear. They pull away because they fear the fire, smoke, and thunder. Afraid of creation's eruption of praise in God's holy presence, they implore Moses to go in their place. The people experience what German philosopher and theologian Rudolph Otto describes as the "mysterium tremendum."[4] Deuteronomy records their terrified response:

> "Behold, the Lord our God has shown us his glory and greatness, and we have heard his voice out of the midst of the fire. This day we have seen God speak with man, and man still live. Now therefore why should we die? For this great fire will consume us. If we hear the voice of the Lord our God any more, we shall die. For who is there of all flesh, that has heard

---

4. Otto, *The Idea of the Holy*, 2nd ed. (Oxford: Oxford University Press, 1950), 12ff.

the voice of the living God speaking out of the midst of the fire as we have, and has still lived? Go near and hear all that the Lord our God will say and speak to us all that the Lord our God will speak to you, and we will hear and do it" (Deuteronomy 5:24–27).

The voice of God speaking His words is too much for the people. The quaking exultation of the earth overwhelms them. They hear the first words of God, which are enough to terrify them. So, Moses alone steps up into the fire and hears: "But you, stand here by me, and I will tell you the whole commandment and the statutes and the rules that you shall teach them" (Deuteronomy 5:31). The people hear the beginning words of worship, but they don't hear all the words as Moses does.

Their fear is so great that when Moses remains on the mountain forty days, receiving the words of worship from God, they think he has perished in the fire. Day after day, they look up at the volcanic explosion of fire on the mountain's peak, breathe the soot from the towers of smoke in the sky, hear the roll of thunder across the desert valley, and determine that Moses has died in the mountain's "death zone."[5] They conclude that he has dissolved in a horrific molten rain, and, in their fear, their hearts return to the relative safety of Egypt.

---

5. The "death zone" describes that stage of a mountain ascent to the summit that is limited in time to accomplish. Any length of time beyond a predetermined projection will likely result in death. For a harrowing description of one expedition's tragic journey through the death zone on Mt. Everest, see Krakauer, *Into Thin Air*.

When the people saw that Moses delayed to come down from the mountain, the people gathered themselves together to Aaron and said to him, "Up, make us gods who shall go before us. As for this Moses, the man who brought us up out of the land of Egypt, we do not know what has become of him" (Exodus 32:1).

The people quickly forge an idol made to look like one of their Egyptian gods. They fashion a golden calf and dance and sing around it, abandoning their calling to be the Lord's priesthood. They return to their old way of worship and the things they learned in Egypt, instead of the new way of worship that God wants to teach them so that they can teach others. They turn back to the comfort of their old-time religion.

> They turn back to the comfort of their old-time religion.

Most of us can relate to their situation because we all are tempted from time to time to return to familiar paths of faith. We seek to worship what is comfortable to us and what we can control. But the God of Sinai cannot be controlled. He is both familiar and unfamiliar. He is what Samuel Terrien calls "the elusive presence."[6] He allows us to know His name while He remains numinous. He lets us hear His voice without seeing His

---

6. Terrien, *The Elusive Presence.*

face. Often, we are like the Israelites and desire a god that we can shape with our own hands. However, God cannot be shaped by us. Rather, He intends to shape us into His image, and for this reason, He is looking for men and women who are fearless and faithful of heart like Moses and want to enter His awesome presence to worship Him. The Lord is looking for men and women who want to step toward the mountain of smoke and fire and be transformed. He is looking for people who want to hear His word, offer Him worship, and go into the world without turning back.

GOD'S WORDS FOR ALL NATIONS

God's words and way of worship are not just for Israel, however. They are for all nations throughout all history. As Israel lived by these words and gave worship to God by obeying them, the world was given an example to follow in their own worship. Rabbis after the time of Jesus interpreted the giving of the commandments in exactly this way. They regarded the Hebrew word *qôlôt (thunder)* as *voices*, and some concluded that God spoke to Moses in the seven voices of all people while others said that God spoke in the seventy voices of the seventy nations.[7] Regardless of whether *qôlôt* represented seven voices or seventy, the rabbis shared a common view of the commandments given at Sinai: They were given by God in the tongues of all the peoples of the world. The

---

7. Skarsaune, *In the Shadow of the Temple*, 396–97.

commandments were given to Israel to model on behalf of the whole world, so that the nations might learn to worship the God of Moses in their own distinctive ways by learning from Israel.

> God's words and way of worship are not just for Israel, however. They are for all nations throughout all history.

SINAI THEOLOGY

God revealed His name and nature to Moses the first time he stepped onto Sinai; He reveals Israel's vocation and calling to Moses the second time. Israel is to be "a kingdom of priests," meaning this nation is to be the worship leader of all nations by living according to the commandments God gives them on the mountain and being an example to the rest of the world on how they might live and worship too. Thus, Israel's vocation is twofold: the people are to worship God by living according to His word to them, and they are to teach the nations how to worship in that very same way.

To lead in worship in the way Moses and Israel are called to do requires faith in God's words and the courage to draw near to Him and to step onto His holy mountain. Sinai worship means to step into God's fiery presence with faith that He will transform us into men and women of worship. It is faith that God's intention toward us is good and not evil and His ambition is for us to praise Him rather than to lament Him. Nonetheless, instead of venturing into a new way of worship by giving all of ourselves to God and His word, we often retreat to familiar ways of worship that don't require as much from us. We turn aside from the mystery and majesty of worship on the mountain to what we ourselves can manage and mold.

To go up into God's presence at Sinai requires a willingness to risk what is familiar and comfortable. The reward will be that we are transfigured like Moses into worshippers who are equipped to help others learn to worship God too.

Reflection and Discussion

1. Why did the Israelites refuse to step onto the mountain with Moses when God drew near to them?
2. What is required of anyone who would enter God's presence to worship Him like Moses?
3. What are you willing to risk in your life to grow in your worship of God?

4

Elijah at Sinai: God's Voice in Silence

THE STORY OF Elijah in the Book of Kings geographically spans the high places (1 Kings 17–2 Kings 2). The first part reaches its climax at the top of Mt. Carmel, where the prophet and his God of Fire overthrow three hundred prophets of Ahab and Jezebel and their god of water. The second part follows Elijah to Mt. Sinai, where he flees Queen Jezebel and her wrath, only to hear God's silence. The story concludes with Elijah leaving the mountain and rocketing skyward in a chariot of fire.

THE DROUGHT OF WORSHIP IN ISRAEL

Elijah's story is one of worship. It begins at a time when the people of Israel, following the lead of Ahab and Jezebel, offer the majority of worship to Baal, the queen's Phoenician god of fresh water. Into this situation, God sends Elijah to prophesy a drought, which is a divine sign of the lack of worship the people are offering to the Lord. Much like the story of the Exodus where Moses demands that Pharaoh let the Israelites worship God, Elijah also confronts an apostate king who has supplanted the worship of *I Am* with that of a foreign deity. Pharaoh refuses to release the Hebrews to worship in the wilderness, and King Ahab impedes worship by building an altar to Baal in Samaria and importing 450 priests of Baal to lead the people in idolatrous rituals. Both stories show the desperation of times without true worship of God by describing the effects of such false worship on the land. In the story of the Exodus, the Nile turns to blood and plagues devastate the country, resulting in suffering and the eventual death of the Egyptians' firstborn sons. In the story of Elijah, a drought afflicts Israel for three years, causing brooks to dry up and poor widows to make plans to die alone with their only sons (1 Kings 17:1–16).

At the end of three long years, Elijah challenges Baal's priests to a contest of fire. Whichever deity responds to the worship given is the one true God. The priests of Baal build an altar, place a sacrifice on it, and call out to him. Nothing happens. There is no fire. In a funny yet sad display, they shout, hop, and cut themselves, hoping to coerce Baal into accepting their sacrifice. It is a futile and destructive exercise in man-made worship. Elijah responds by building an altar, placing a bull on it, and pouring water over both. He saturates the altar and sacrifice with water, symbolically covering everything with the veneer of Baal (the Phoenician god of fresh water). Immediately, a storm of fire falls from the sky, incinerating the sacrifice and evaporating the water. In the process, Baal ceases to exist. Elijah's God is the God of fire, water, and the whole earth. He alone is deserving of worship.[1] Just as the drought of rain represented the drought of worship among the people, and the frantic, self-mutilating behavior of Baal's priests on Mt. Carmel represented the destructive nature of self-made worship, so also the return of the rains represents the return of worship in Israel. From this event, we learn that worship brings replenishment and blessing to God's people. This replenishment anticipates much later "times of refreshing" that people will experience when they turn to Jesus and acknowledge (worship) Him as the "Holy and Righteous One" (Acts 3:13–14, 19–21).

> From this event, we learn that worship brings replenishment and blessing to God's people.

THE SILENCE OF SINAI

The story moves from Mt. Carmel to Mt. Sinai and reprises the narrative of the Exodus in several ways.[2] The most obvious resemblance is that both stories feature prophets climbing Mt. Sinai after fleeing angry monarchs. Pharaoh

---

1. *Yah* is an abbreviated form of *Yahweh*, the covenant name of God, which is present in Elijah's own name, which means "My God is Yah."
2. See Victor P. Hamilton's comparison in Hamilton, *Handbook on the Historical Books*, 433. Thanks to Sean Sams, a graduate of The King's University and Registrar at Valor College, for this reference.

chases Moses into the wilderness, only to drown in the Red Sea. Jezebel hunts Elijah after the debacle on Mt. Carmel, only to be devoured by dogs (1 Kings 21:23–24). Along the way, both prophets receive miraculous provision from God. Moses and the Israelites eat manna from heaven and drink water from a rock as they make their way to the mountain. God feeds them with "a fine, flake-like thing, fine as frost on the ground" (Exodus 16:14). In the same way, God feeds Elijah with a cake and quenches his thirst with water from a jar. The cake and water provided by God sustain Elijah through the wilderness where he travels for forty days, which corresponds to Moses' forty years in the wilderness (1 Kings 19:6–8).

At Sinai, Moses receives the commandments of the covenant and God's guidelines for worship in fire and thunder. Elijah doesn't receive any commandments, however. He only hears "a low whisper" (*qol demamah daqqāh*) (1 Kings 19:12). The fact that Elijah receives no further commandments signifies that what God gave to Moses remains in effect. God doesn't add even one word to what He has said to Moses. In fact, He doesn't say anything at all. According to Old Testament scholar William Dumbrell, the Hebrew is better translated as "the voice of drawn out silence."[3] Elijah has gone to the mountain of Moses to hear God's voice, but he doesn't hear any words.

The silence he hears is God's divine response to his despair. Elijah believes that he alone has been faithful to

---

3. Dumbrell, 98.

the *I Am* of Israel. He is convinced that only he has
remained true to worship.

> The silence he hears is
> God's divine response
> to his despair.

"I have been very jealous for the Lord, the God of
hosts. For the people of Israel have forsaken your
covenant, thrown down your altars, and killed your
prophets with the sword, and I, only I, am left"
(1 Kings 19:10).

After his zealous and violent defense of God, Elijah feels
abandoned and bewildered. He is so dejected that, like
Moses, he asks God to take his life.[4] And it is in the midst
of his complaint that he experiences a tornado force wind,
an earthquake, and a fire, not unlike Moses' experience
of thunder, lightning, smoke, and fire on the mountain.
But God doesn't speak to Elijah in the same way that He
spoke to Moses. To Moses, the Lord spoke in ear-covering
loudness: "And as the sound of the trumpet grew louder and
louder,... God answered [Moses] in thunder" (Exodus 19:19).
To Elijah, He speaks in ear-piercing quietness:

> The Lord passed by, and a great and strong wind
> tore the mountains and broke in pieces the rocks
> before the Lord, but the Lord was not in the wind.
> And after the wind an earthquake, but the Lord was
> not in the earthquake. And after the earthquake a

---

4. Hamilton, 434.

fire, but the Lord was not in the fire. And after the fire the sound of a low whisper (1 Kings 19:11–12).

Both Moses and Elijah hear God speak in a cleft on Mt. Sinai. Moses hears God in thunder, so we expect the same for Elijah. But Elijah doesn't hear the Lord in the wind or the earthquake or even the fire; he hears Him in the silence. Elijah's experience is antiphonic to that of Moses. What we learn from these two stories is that God speaks from Mt. Sinai in all types of ways and in all types of voices. He even speaks in all types of languages.[5] On the mountain, God speaks in the loudest of voices as well as in no voice at all. He whispers in thunder and shouts in silence.

> On the mountain, God speaks in the loudest of voices as well as in no voice at all. He whispers in thunder and shouts in silence.

The silence in Elijah's ears represents the eternal veracity and creative power of God's word. What God has said, He has said. As Isaiah reports, the word that God speaks always fulfills His desires: "[My word] shall not return to me empty but it shall accomplish that which I purpose and shall succeed in the thing for which I sent it" (Isaiah 55:11).

---

5. As noted above, the rabbis believed that God spoke from Sinai in all the languages of the world.

THE WORSHIP OF 7,000

In the silence, Elijah hears God's question, "What are you doing here?" and His command, "Return on your way to the wilderness of Damascus. And when you arrive, you shall anoint Hazael to be king over Syria" (1 Kings 19:13, 15). Just as Moses' visit to the mountain resulted in a calling to lead the nations in the worship of the Lord, Elijah's visit results in the appointment of a new king over one of those nations to do God's will. Hazael is one of three men Elijah anoints to judge by the sword those who have not been faithful to God. It is a violent act that recalls the judgment of the sword upon the Israelites after Moses descended the mountain only to find the people worshipping the golden calf. Three thousand men were put to death that day. The author of Kings does not tell how many were killed by Hazael for their apostasy. *The point of the story is not how many failed to worship God but how many remained faithful in their devotion to Him.* In fact, 7,000 men survive this judgment because they did not bend their knees to Baal. Through this event, Elijah sees that he is not the only man who has been faithful in his worship during this desperate time. Others like him have been faithful in their worship too. At the first Sinai, Moses went up the mountain to learn the way of worship by himself as the people remained behind. At the second Sinai, Elijah goes up to discover that he is not the only worshipper of God, but there are 7,000 others who worship God and God alone.

SINAI THEOLOGY

The God of Sinai is a God of fire who speaks to His people in very different ways. Sometimes He thunders. Other times He whispers. Only those who have climbed Sinai like Elijah and have devoted themselves completely to God, and God alone, will hear Him speak His words in silence.

> The God of Sinai is a God of fire who speaks to His people in very different ways. Sometimes He thunders. Other times He whispers.

What we learn from Sinai is that the worship God desires results in blessing for His people. The blessing may not come right away as in the story of Elijah (1 Kings 18:41–46). It may take time, and when it comes, it may look like a small cloud in a blue sky (18:44). Even so, just as the blessing of worship brought rains of renewal, replenishment, and refreshment to the Israelites through the worship given by Elijah, so too will our worship of God bring renewal to our lives.

Reflection and Discussion

1. What did the drought at the time of Elijah represent?
2. Why did Elijah pour water over the sacrifice that he offered to God?
3. Has God ever spoken to you in a loud way? Has He ever spoken to you in silence?

5

Jeremiah's Experience of Sinai: Fire in the Bones

OF ALL THE prophets in the Old Testament, only Elijah and Moses make their way through the wilderness to Mt. Sinai.[1] There is no record of Isaiah or Ezekiel climbing the mountain. There is no account of Hosea, Micah, Zechariah, or Malachi ascending fiery Sinai to hear God's words. Amos travels north to Israel from his home in Tekoa in the south to prophesy; Jonah boards a boat and sails west to Tarshish to flee God's word; Habakkuk stands on the ramparts of the walls of Jerusalem to look out east over the armies of Babylon and see what God will do. All of these men hear the word of the Lord without ever journeying into the wilderness and climbing the mountain.

Jeremiah is representative of these prophets. He doesn't travel to Mt. Sinai to hear from the Lord. He

---

1. That Moses is regarded as the first prophet in Israel can be seen in Deuteronomy, where Moses himself says, "The Lord your God will raise up for you a prophet like me from among you." and God confirms, "I will raise up for them a prophet like you from among their brothers. And I will put my words in his mouth, and he shall speak to them all that I command him" (Deuteronomy 18:15, 18).

doesn't ascend the smoking mountain. Instead, he remains in Jerusalem and hears God's word in the midst of siege and struggle. He speaks a divine word to king, priest, prophet, and people during a time of great turbulence as the armies of Babylon camp around the capital city. Jeremiah's message is an unpopular one that sounds like defeat and surrender. By the time the Babylonians are finished, the walls of the city will be rubble, the temple a pile of broken stones, and the king's eyes blinded.[2] Jeremiah's predicament is impossible. Outside the city stand the merciless Babylonians while inside the city the leaders and people refuse to reckon with their ways that have led to this terror-filled moment.

THE TEMPLE AS A TALISMAN

The word Jeremiah speaks denounces idolatry and urges fidelity. He warns of famine, pestilence, and impending exile unless the people change their way of worship. His message will "tingle the ears" of those who hear news of the divine disaster that will come upon the people of Israel for their idolatry:

> "Because the people have forsaken me and have profaned this place by making offerings in it to other gods whom neither they nor their fathers nor the kings of Judah have known; and because they have

---

2. Though some scholars have minimized the effects of the exile, the evidence describes a period of upheaval and personal and societal destruction.

filled this place with the blood of innocents, and
have built the high places of Baal to burn their sons
in the fire as burnt offerings to Baal, which I did not
command or decree, nor did it come into my mind ...
I will make this city a horror" (Jeremiah 19:4–5, 8).

The people are offering sacrifices to foreign gods. They
are ignoring the true worship of God and the keeping of
His commandments and participating in the convenient
and superficial worship of idols (Jeremiah 3:6–10; 7:8–11;
16:16–20; 17:1–3). But they are not worried because they
still have the temple! God's house has become a false
talisman to them. They believe it will protect them from
the consequences of their behavior. Jeremiah warns that
the sanctuary will not save them from God's judgment for
idolatry and their disregard for His ways. He admonishes,
"Do not trust in these deceptive words: 'This is the temple
of the Lord, the temple of the Lord, the temple of the
Lord'" (Jeremiah 7:4). The temple will not protect them
from disregarding the commands God has given them.

> God's house has become a
> false talisman to them. They
> believe it will protect them from the
> consequences of their behavior.

"Behold, you trust in deceptive words to no avail.
Will you steal, murder, commit adultery, swear
falsely, make offerings to Baal, and go after other
gods that you have not known, and then come and
stand before me in this house, which is called by
my name, and say 'We are delivered'—only to go on

doing all these abominations? Has this house, which is called by my name, become a den of robbers in your eyes?" (Jeremiah 7:8–11).

For this idolatry and false worship, God will fight like a Divine Warrior against His people on the side of the Babylonians.[3] The only shred of hope they have is to surrender to God by giving themselves over to their enemies.

> "Behold, I set before you the way of life and the way of death. He who stays in this city shall die by the sword, by famine, and by pestilence, but he who goes out and surrenders to the Chaldeans who are besieging you shall live and shall have his life as a prize of war. For I have set my face against this city for harm and not for good" (Jeremiah 21:8–9).[4]

Why God's judgment for idolatry? Why the threat of exile? God's calling to Israel has not changed. The people are to be a kingdom of priests. They are to lead the nations in worship by living according to God's words given at Sinai. They are to abide by the commandments and in their life with one another and in their worship of God show the nations, like Babylon, who God is and what His worship looks like. If Israel will not do that in the land God had given to them as a gift, then God will place them in those very nations to be a witness to the people there.

---

3. Longman III, and Dillard, *Introduction to the Old Testament*, 73, 352. See also Longman, III, "The Divine Warrior," 290–307.
4. See also Jeremiah 38:2, 38:17–20.

REJECTING SINAI'S WORDS

For speaking this word of submission, interpreted as traitorous by the leaders and people of Jerusalem, Jeremiah is beaten by the high priest, placed in the city stocks, and denounced by family and friends. Instead of standing on the mountain as others have, he finds himself clamped down by a heavy yoke of iron and wood. In his anguish, Jeremiah cries out to the Lord and says that he has been deceived. He has become a laughingstock to everyone.

> For whenever I speak, I cry out,
>> I shout, "Violence and destruction!"
> For the word of the Lord has become
>> for me,
>> a reproach and derision all day long.
> If I say, "I will not mention him,
>> or speak any more in his name,"
> there is in my heart as it were a burning fire
>> shut up in my bones,
> and I am weary with holding it in,
>> and I cannot (Jeremiah 20:8–9).

The consuming fire of Mt. Sinai has come to Jeremiah and burns within him in such a way that he *cannot not* speak the words of the Lord. The mountain of God's revelation has been uprooted and planted in the prophet's heart and mind, and he has no choice but to shout the words reverberating within him. Even as God gave His name to Israel when He brought them out of Egypt so they would know who they worshipped at the mountain, so also Jeremiah must remind Israel of that same name as the mountain comes to them through his messages.

God is calling His people to account for their self-serving worship. But no one wants to hear it. Like the Israelites who drew away from the mountain where God spoke in thunder, the people and leaders of Jerusalem do not want to hear the words that God speaks through Jeremiah. Pashur the priest beats Jeremiah to silence him; the prophet Hananiah publicly refutes his words of judgment; King Jehoiakim cuts a scroll containing Jeremiah's words into ribbons and burns them in his winter fire; King Zedekiah throws him into a well where he "[sinks] in the mud" and his words cannot be heard.[5] None of these men want to be near the mountain fire of God's words delivered through Jeremiah.

> God is calling His people to account for their self-serving worship. But no one wants to hear it.

Still, whether in wooden stocks, the middle of an angry crowd, or sunk in the mud of a dank cistern, the fire of Sinai and words of the mountain cannot be contained within Jeremiah. They will be heard, and so the prophet despairs:

> Cursed be the day
> on which I was born!

---

5. Jeremiah 20:1–2; 26:1–9; 28:1–4; 36:9–26; 38:1–6.

The day when my mother bore me,
  let it not be blessed!
Cursed be the man who brought the news to
my father....
Let that man be like the cities
  that the Lord overthrew without pity;
let him hear a cry in the morning
  and an alarm at noon,
because he did not kill me in the womb;
  so my mother would have been my
  grave (Jeremiah 20:14–17).

Like Moses and Elijah before him, Jeremiah is tempted to think that death is preferable to the awesome responsibility that comes with the revelation of God's word. A later biblical writer will declare that God is a consuming fire who will burn out any vestige of self that remains in the man or woman who touches Sinai or, like Jeremiah, is touched in his heart by the mountain (Hebrews 12:29).

JESUS AND THE TIMES OF JEREMIAH

Jesus recalls the times of Jeremiah when He enters the temple and overturns the tables of the money changers and vendors who sell animals for sacrifice. He decries what He sees and quotes from both Jeremiah and Isaiah when He says, "Is it not written, 'My house shall be called a house of prayer for all the nations'? But you have made it a den of robbers" (Mark 11:17; Jeremiah 7:11; Isaiah 56:7). Jesus' word that the temple is for all people helps us appreciate

His motives for overturning the tables and gives us insight into the significance of Jeremiah's message for Him.

It is thought that several years before Jesus began His ministry, the high priests had moved the vendors and money changers from outside the temple precincts into the Court of the Gentiles, where the necessary business of the temple was conducted. This was done for the sake of efficiency. It was easier and saved time for pilgrims to change their money and buy animals for sacrifice inside the temple rather than outside. Because the temple kept all its money reserves in coins minted in Tyre, money changers were needed to exchange the coins from various cities and provinces into Tyrian ones. Pilgrims from distant places then purchased their animals for sacrifice from licensed vendors with Tyrian money and offer them to the priests. Jesus doesn't dispute the service provided by the money changers or the vendors. He knows that pilgrims need such things.[6] What He disputes is the disruption of worship in the Court of the Gentiles. Gentile men and women from all over the Mediterranean world and other lands had nowhere else to go if they wanted to offer worship to Israel's God. But how could they worship when all they heard and smelled were the animals? How could they focus on the Lord God if all they heard were coins dropping onto metal scales? How could they direct their attention to the one true God when they heard men arguing over exchange rates and the cost of animals?

---

6. Even so, Jesus would have rejected the use of Tyrian coins because of the image of Phoenician god Melqart that they bore.

Where else could they go to give honor to the God of Abraham, Isaac, and Jacob? Jesus is filled with grief over the fact that Israel, which has been given the privilege of leading the nations in worship, is obstructing the worship of those very nations and making it difficult for them to do so. He sees that the temple and its custodians are not serving the priestly role for which God had delivered Israel from Egypt to perform and brought back from Babylonian exile to accomplish. Temple authorities are not leading the nations in worship. With all this in mind, Jesus says the temple is to be a place of prayer—a place of worship—for all the nations, but it has been turned into a mere place of business.

> Jesus is filled with grief over the fact that Israel, which has been given the privilege of leading the nations in worship, is obstructing the worship of those very nations and making it difficult for them to do so.

Jesus sees the same thing happening that Jeremiah saw in his day. The temple had become a false talisman of worship. Temple leaders were making the temple into a place of transaction rather than a center for transformative worship. In Jeremiah's day, the people went up to the temple believing that their participation in its rituals and festivals brought about salvation. It didn't matter that as they did so they also oppressed the sojourner, neglected the orphan, ignored the widow, and indulged foreign gods. Jeremiah saw that people felt safe in the temple, even though they were stealing, murdering, committing adultery, swearing falsely, and giving offerings to Baal (Jeremiah 7:9–10). They had turned away from the covenant by not keeping its commandments. The people

> "have turned back to the iniquities of their forefathers, who refused to hear my words. They have gone after other gods to serve [worship] them. The house of Israel and the house of Judah have broken my covenant that I made with their fathers" (11:9–10).

The people at the times of both Jesus and Jeremiah act in a similar way to the first Exodus generation that God had brought out of the "iron furnace" (Jeremiah 11:4).[7] Those people forged a golden calf when they thought Moses had perished on the mountain. Jeremiah's generation believed their dutiful temple attendance and sacrifices would secure their safety and protect them from the Babylonians, but like the priestly elites of Jesus' day, they impeded the worship of God by the nations. What Jesus and Jeremiah understood, but the people and their leaders did not, was that Israel's failure to worship God in faithfulness to the words of His covenant and in purity as a priesthood meant they were not leading nations like Rome and Babylon in true worship.

---

7. The reference to "iron furnace" is a specific recollection of Israel's servitude in Egypt. See also Deuteronomy 4:20.

SINAI IN THE HEART

God's message to the people of Judah through Jeremiah is not solely one of judgment, however. It also includes the promise of the covenant revitalized. The Lord declares,

> "The days are coming ... when I will make a new covenant with the house of Israel and the house of Judah, not like the covenant that I made with their fathers on the day when I took them by the hand to bring them out of the land of Egypt.... This is the covenant that I will make with the house of Israel after those days:... I will put my law within them, and I will write it on their hearts" (Jeremiah 31:31–33).

Jeremiah sees a future day when God will put His words within all His people in the same way He has put them in Jeremiah. Just as God placed His words in Jeremiah that burned like fire, so also will He place the words of His law inside Israel. This means they will all experience the fire of Mt. Sinai in their lives. Jeremiah's new covenant is nothing less than the movement of the mountain of God's revealed word into the hearts of all His people. It is the fire of Sinai in the bones.

Jeremiah's new covenant is nothing less than the movement of the mountain of God's revealed word into the hearts of all His people. It is the fire of Sinai in the bones.

Two of Jesus' disciples experience this fire of Sinai in their hearts on the day of His resurrection. According to Luke, these disciples were making their way to Emmaus, west of Jerusalem, while discussing the tragic events of the past few days. Their hearts were numb with the loss and fear felt over Jesus' crucifixion. As they are going on their way, Jesus, unrecognized, joins in their conversation. They tell him, "We had hoped that he was the one to redeem Israel," as they recount the women's report of the empty tomb. In response, Jesus exclaims that they are "slow of heart" and what they have reported was foretold by Moses and the prophets. After Jesus departs, the disciples say, "Did not our hearts burn within us while he talked to us on the road, while he opened to us the Scriptures?" (Luke 24:13–32). Their hearts burned with God's revelatory words spoken by Jesus concerning His death and resurrection in the Scriptures. They felt what Jeremiah felt when God spoke His eternal word into the prophet's heart.

The result of hearing God's word in one's heart is the ability to know Him.

> "I will be their God, and they shall be my people. And no longer shall each one teach his neighbor and each his brother, saying, 'Know the Lord,' for they shall all know me, from the least of them to the greatest.... For I will forgive their iniquity, and I will remember their sin no more" (Jeremiah 31:33–34).

Jeremiah says that "all" will know the Lord. What is true for the people of Israel will be true for all nations through Israel's witness of worship. *All* will know God's word, and rather than teach one another, they will worship in the freedom of forgiveness that God offers.

SINAI ON THE LIPS

Not only does God burn the fire of Sinai upon Jeremiah's heart, but He also burns it upon Isaiah's mouth. From the altar before God's throne, an angel takes a coal and sears the prophet's lips to purify him so that he might speak God's words. Isaiah is a man of unclean lips living among a people of unclean lips and in need of purification. No one in Israel is worthy to speak God's message. Yet, to this man at worship in God's temple, God gives the gift of His word for the people. Who will go for God? The prophet who has been cleansed in worship will go and speak the message God wants spoken. As with Jeremiah, Isaiah will find the people unreceptive to his words. They will "keep on hearing, but ... not understand; keep on seeing, but ... not perceive" (Isaiah 6:9). Nonetheless, he will speak them. God's word cannot be contained.

Isaiah's experience is not unlike Jeremiah's fire in the bones or that of the disciples on the day of Pentecost. Luke reports that the disciples were in the temple worshiping God for His generous provision when they were touched by fire and compelled by the Spirit to go to Judea, Samaria, and all the nations. The tongues of fire upon the disciples signify the purity of speech by which they will proclaim God's message to all people. Who will go for God to the nations? *Israel, in the form of the disciples, will go* as men and women purified by the Spirit. It is for this reason that

Peter quotes from the prophet Joel in his Pentecost sermon: "In the last days it shall be, God declares, that I will pour out my Spirit on all flesh, and your sons and your daughters shall prophesy ... in those days I will pour out my Spirit, and they shall prophesy" (Acts 2:17–18; Joel 2:28–32). To prophesy is a privilege given to sons and daughters who have been delivered from bondage to receive God's word for worship among the nations at the mountain. The fire of the mountain has purified Isaiah to take God's word to His people Israel and, through them, to the nations.

> To prophesy is a privilege given to sons and daughters who have been delivered from bondage to receive God's word for worship among the nations at the mountain.

SINAI THEOLOGY

Jeremiah experiences the fire of Sinai in his life when God places His word deep inside him. The power of that word is so strong that the prophet must declare it, even though it sounds like despair and defeat and will be rejected by the nation's leaders, people, and even Jeremiah's family. But the word that sounds like despair and defeat is in truth a word of hope that calls Judah back to the exclusive worship of God and fidelity to His commandments. It is through such worship and obedience that Israel will fulfill her vocation to God and her mission to the world.

Isaiah experiences Sinai's fire when an angel touches his lips with a coal from God's altar so he can speak God's words to the people, calling them back to faithful observance of His commandments and way of worship. He is purified by the fire of the altar because the words he will speak are pure and will minister to the hard hearts of a people very much like Israel when they left Egypt, needing to be made pure by the word God gave to them at the mountain.

To live with God's word deep inside us and to have it seared on our lips is to experience the power and purity of Sinai. It is God's desire that our hearts and lips be touched with the fire of the mountain as were Jeremiah and Isaiah. God desires that His word so fills our lives and our mouths that when we speak, we speak truth, love, and compassion to everyone around us, calling them into a profound, abiding relationship of worship with God.

Reflection and Discussion

1. What does Jeremiah mean when he says that God will write His covenant on the hearts of His people?
2. Why does Jesus overturn tables in the temple?
3. Have you ever experienced something like Jeremiah's fire in his bones?

6

Jesus on Sinai

THROUGHOUT HIS GOSPEL, Matthew shows that Jesus is a new and greater Moses by locating Him on mountains at key moments throughout His ministry. These passages represent Matthew's mountaintop theology of Jesus (Matthew 4:8–11; 5:1–7:27; 17:1–8; 24:3–25:46; 28:16–20).

THE MOUNTAINS OF TEMPTATION AND ASCENSION

Jesus' first mountaintop experience occurs during the wilderness temptation when He is confronted by the devil. Matthew records that after being tempted to turn stones into loaves of bread and then to jump off the pinnacle of the temple, Jesus is urged to bow down and worship the devil:

> Again, the devil took him to a very high mountain and showed him all the kingdoms of the world and their glory. And he said to him, "All these I will give you, if you will fall down and worship me." Then Jesus said to him, "Be gone, Satan! For it is written, 'You shall worship the Lord your God and him only shall you serve'" (Matthew 4:8–10).

Matthew does not record the location of this mountain or its name. We only know that it is a wilderness mountain where the worship of God by the nations is the primary concern. In this way, it resembles Mt. Sinai, where Israel was called to lead the nations in worship as God's priesthood. Jesus' response to the devil reprises Moses' word to Israel: "It is the Lord your God you shall fear. Him you shall serve [worship] and by His name you shall swear" (Deuteronomy 6:13). Moses exhorted the people to worship because that is why God brought them out of Egypt (Deuteronomy 5:1–21; 6:4–9, 12–13). Their worship was to be a witness to the nations of their recognition of God's great work in their lives.

This temptation reveals that Jesus entered the world as a prophet like Moses and a brother to Israel (Deuteronomy 18:15–18) to gain the nations and their glory for His Father. He will not fulfill this purpose by bowing to the devil, however, but by bowing to the Father's will, which involves going the way of the cross. This is confirmed by Matthew at the end of his Gospel in the Great Commission, where we hear Jesus say on another mountain:

> "All authority in heaven and on earth has been given to me. Go therefore and make disciples of all nations, baptizing them in the name of the Father and of the Son and of the Holy Spirit, teaching them to observe all that I have commanded you" (Matthew 28:18–20).

Jesus is empowered with all authority because He accomplished the will of His Father and held fast to the words His Father spoke at the Jordan—"You are My beloved Son." As a result of His faithfulness to those words, Jesus is able to pass that authority on to His followers. The charge to take the good news to the nations, given to Jesus' disciples at His ascension, is the same call given to Israel at Mt. Sinai—to lead the nations in the worship of God. The first and last mountains in Matthew's Gospel reveal that worship involves keeping God's word, submitting to His will, and possessing the authority to see His presence cleanse the nations through baptism so they themselves may approach Him in worship too. [1]

> The first and last mountains in Matthew's Gospel reveal that worship involves keeping God's word, submitting to His will, and possessing the authority to see His presence cleanse the nations through baptism so they themselves may approach Him in worship too.

THE MOUNT OF TRANSFIGURATION

All three Synoptic Gospels record the transfiguration of Jesus on a mountain (Matthew 17:1–8; Mark 9:2–8; Luke 9:28–36). They report that Jesus takes Peter, James,

---

1. Pastor Jack Hayford draws out the relationship between the worship of God and the exercise of His authority in his book, *The Reward of Worship.*

and John with Him to "a high mountain" where He is clothed in God's glory. The mountain is not named and cannot be the actual Mt. Sinai since the former is likely located somewhere in Galilee.[2] Nonetheless, it is certainly a symbol of Sinai, given that Jesus meets Moses and Elijah there. He meets with the only two men in history who had definitive encounters with God on that wilderness mountain.

Matthew particularly regards the mountain as another Sinai. One of his objectives in writing his Gospel is to show Jesus to be a new Moses. For this reason, he reports the trip to Egypt that Joseph and Mary take when Herod seeks the death of their son, and along with Luke, he describes the temptation of Jesus in the wilderness in such a way as to recall Israel's forty years in the desert. Here, the transfiguration and the story of the epileptic boy that follows recall the story of Moses on Sinai and the making of the golden calf (Exodus 19–20, 32).

Matthew writes that while on the mountain Jesus' face "shone like the sun and his clothes became white as light" (Matthew 17:2). The glory of God radiates from Him not unlike the manner it did from Moses as he descended the mountain after receiving the commandments from God.

> "When Moses came down from Mount Sinai, with
> the two tablets of the testimony in his hand ... [he]
> did not know that the skin of his face shone because
> he had been talking with God. Aaron and all the

---

2. Many believe the mountain was Mt. Hermon in northern Galilee, the highest mountain in Israel at 9,232 feet.

people of Israel saw Moses, and behold, the skin of his face shone, and they were afraid to come near him" (Exodus 34:29–30).

So great was the glory of God upon Moses that he had to wear a veil over his face to protect the people from its blinding light.

> "Whenever Moses went in before the Lord to speak with him, he would remove the veil, until he came out. And when he came out and told the people of Israel what he was commanded, the people of Israel would see the face of Moses, that the skin of Moses' face was shining. And Moses would put the veil over his face again until he went in to speak with him" (Exodus 34:34–35).

Jesus is covered with the glory of God in a manner similar to Moses, except that it is not just His face that shines. Jesus' entire being radiates with glory. It is no wonder the disciples prostrate themselves before Him in worship. If the Israelites were afraid to approach Moses because his face gleamed with glory, how much more will the disciples be filled with awe when Jesus' body is enfolded with divine brilliance? A bright cloud then appears, and a voice speaks out of it: "This is my beloved Son, with whom I am well pleased; listen to him." The sound of the voice is so great and startling that the disciples fall to the ground in fear and reverence.[3]

---

3. The Scriptures do not record anything about Joshua's reaction when he went up Sinai with Moses, but it's likely the awe of God in him would have been much like that experienced by Peter, James, and John.

Jesus is covered with the glory of God in a manner similar to Moses, except that it is not just His face that shines. Jesus' entire being radiates with glory.

Often, the transfiguration is interpreted as an event that shows Jesus to be the fulfillment of the law and the prophets. Moses is representative of the law, having received it from God on Sinai, and Elijah is representative of the prophets who remained faithful to God's word despite the unbelief and opposition of others to that word. Jesus is seen as a prophet who continues the faithfulness to God's word begun by Moses and maintained by Elijah.

This understanding of Jesus as a continuation of Moses and the prophets should not keep us from seeing Jesus' transfiguration as a wholly new Sinai event. He is on the mountain in a bright cloud with blinding light when a heavenly voice commands His disciples to listen to Him. God doesn't speak new commandments like those given to Moses. He doesn't speak confidentially about new assignments like those issued to Elijah. He simply says to *listen* to His beloved Son. Jesus' words are to be regarded at least at the same level as those spoken by Moses and Elijah.

One cannot help but detect here an allusion to the Shema:[4]

---

4. The word *Shema* is an imperative Hebrew verb that means *listen*. "Hear, O Israel," means "Listen, Israel."

"Hear, O Israel: The Lord our God, the Lord is one. You shall love the Lord your God with all your heart and with all your soul and with all your might. And these [commandments] that I command you today shall be on your heart. You shall teach them diligently to your children and shall talk of them when you sit in your house, and when you walk by the way, and when you lie down, and when you rise. You shall bind them as a sign on your hand, and they shall be as frontlets between your eyes. You shall write them on the doorposts of your house and on your gates" (Deuteronomy 6:4–9).

Here on the mountain, God declares, "Hear, O Israel" to the disciples of Jesus, and just as Israel was exhorted by Moses at Sinai to keep God's commandments with all of their being and to talk about them with their children and one another all the time, wherever they are, in everything they do, and in all their thoughts, the disciples are to do the same. They are to *hear* Jesus with their hearts all the time, wherever they are, in everything they do, and in all that they think. Just as the words of Sinai were words for all of life, so also Jesus' words are for all people; they are words are words for home and for city; for night and for day; for work and for rest; and they are words for thought and for reflection. This is what God means when He says to the disciples, "Listen to Jesus." Worship begins with listening and obedience to the words that Jesus speaks. [5]

---

5. Klaus Bockmuehl observes that listening involves obedience: "The Latin verb *obaudire*, 'to listen,' is the origin of the English word *obedience*. In a profound way, and whether we realize it or not, listening

Worship begins with listening and obedience to the words that Jesus speaks.

MUSTARD-SEED FAITH AND SINAI

The connection between Jesus' transfiguration and Sinai is strengthened by the story that follows Jesus' descent from the mountain. All three Synoptic Gospels report the deliverance of a boy suffering with epilepsy. When Jesus descends the mountain, He looks upon a chaotic scene very much like that which Moses saw when he came down from Mt. Sinai with Joshua. A distressed father asks Jesus to deliver his son from the seizures because the disciples have failed to do so. Jesus responds in a manner that many have interpreted as impatient and angry when He says, "O faithless and twisted generation, how long am I to be with you?" (Matthew 17:17; Luke 9:41).

Jesus may have indeed been frustrated with the disciples, but His frustration is with their unbelief, which resembles that of the Exodus generation in the wilderness. When He says, "faithless and twisted generation" (*genea apistos kai diestrammenē*), He specifically links their behavior with that of the first-generation Israelites whom Moses led out of Egypt. Thus, Jesus is not expressing disappointment and saying, "You're

___

is a form of obedience." Bockmuehl, *Listening to the God Who Speaks,* 145.

hopeless," or "When will you ever learn?" He is identifying them as people who are not responding with faith to the signs God is giving them through His ministry, just as Israel failed to respond with faith to the signs God gave them through Moses.

When the disciples ask Jesus why they couldn't deliver the boy from the demon, He says their "little faith" is the obstacle.[6] He then says that if they had faith like a mustard seed, they would be able to move "this" mountain from which He has just descended (Matthew 17:20–21). But aren't mustard seeds small, too? What is the difference between "little faith" and "mustard seed faith"?

Matthew records several stories in which Jesus calls the disciples "little faith ones." For instance, He does so in the Sermon on the Mount when He cautions them against anxiety over things such as food and clothing.

> "If God so clothes the grass of the field, which today is alive and tomorrow is thrown into the oven, will he not much more clothe you, O you of little faith? Therefore do not be anxious, saying, 'What shall we eat?' or 'What shall we drink?' … But seek first the kingdom of God and his righteousness, and all these things will be added to you" (Matthew 6:30–33).

Here, a "little faith one" is a person who gives more energy and attention to the necessities of life than to knowing God's ways (righteousness) and doing His will (God's kingdom).

---

6. The Greek word for "little faith" is *oligopistian*.

Here, a "little faith one" is a person who gives more energy and attention to the necessities of life than to knowing God's ways (righteousness) and doing His will (God's kingdom).

Later, when the disciples find themselves in a deadly storm on the Sea of Galilee, they rouse Jesus from sleep and shout over the shrieking wind, "Save us, Lord, we are perishing!" Jesus shouts back, "Why are you afraid, O you of little faith?" *Why are they afraid?* They fear a watery death in the storm! Does Jesus belittle their fear by calling them men of "little faith"? No, He calls attention to their preoccupation with the wind, waves, and sea spray in their faces (Matthew 8:23–27). Little faith ones are those who feel powerless in the midst of extreme circumstances.

Possibly the most perplexing reference to little faith by Jesus is in relation to Peter. When the bold disciple sees Jesus walking on the surface of the Sea of Galilee late one night, Peter responds to Jesus' invitation to join Him on the sea by getting out of the boat and walking on the water. Matthew reports,

> So Peter got out of the boat and walked on the water and came to Jesus. But when he saw the wind, he was afraid, and beginning to sink he cried out, "Lord, save me." Jesus immediately reached out his hand and took hold of him, saying to him, "O you of little faith, why did you doubt?" (Matthew 14:29–31).

We may wonder at Jesus' response to Peter in this moment. After all, he was the only disciple to venture out in the great wind and walk toward Jesus on the water. No one else stepped outside of the boat. Yet, a closer look reveals that Peter began to sink when the wind blew away the word of command that Jesus had given to him: "when he saw the wind, he was afraid" (Matthew 14:30). A little faith man or woman forgets the word of the Lord when confronted by the storms of life.[7]

Little faith focuses on both the small and big things of life. It becomes consumed with life's necessities and overwhelmed by its crises. Like Israel in the wilderness, when confronted with need and crisis, the disciples focus on their needs and desperate circumstances. Israel didn't have food or water, so in fear they grumbled and complained. They claimed God intended to harm them. Likewise, the disciples find themselves in difficult circumstances and voice their fears. "Don't you care if we perish?" They act just like the Israelites in the wilderness, which is why Jesus describes them as a "faithless and twisted generation."[8]

A mustard-seed mindset is altogether different. It is a mindset that remembers the words spoken by God. To understand this, all we need to do is to look at a brief story Jesus told about a mustard seed:

---

7. In this way, a little faith person is much like the rocky soil in Jesus' parable of the sower. The individual receives the teaching of God's word but allows daily cares, tribulations, or persecutions to choke out the life that God's word brings. See Matthew 13:1–9, 18–23.
8. The Greek word that is translated *twisted* (*diastrephō*) means to mislead as well as twist or pervert.

"The kingdom of heaven is like a grain of mustard seed that a man took and sowed in his field. It is the smallest of all seeds, but when it has grown it is larger than all the garden plants and becomes a tree, so that the birds of the air come and make nests in its branches" (Matthew 13:31–32).

A mustard-seed mindset is altogether different. It is a mindset that remembers the words spoken by God.

In this parable, Jesus compares God's will (the kingdom of heaven) with the planting of a small seed in a field. It is easy to overlook the allusion He makes to God's great Sinai-call to Israel: the man who plants the smallest seed that grows into a tree for birds to roost is none other than God Himself who planted His small people Israel. "It was not because you were more in number than any other people that the Lord set his love on you and chose you, for you were the fewest of all peoples" (Deuteronomy 7:7). The Lord placed them in a new land to be a witness to all the nations who would flock to them and make a home with them when they saw how much He had blessed them. Jesus says this is God's will—for His people to live by His word and offer worship to Him in such a way that testifies of His goodness to the world. God put His eternal purpose into motion at Sinai.

When Jesus tells His disciples that they can move "this" mountain "from here to there" with mustard-seed faith, He means that they can see God's Sinai purpose manifest itself wherever they are as they receive and act upon the word that He speaks. He means that the revelation given and the relationship established at Sinai will go with His sons and daughters from here to there as they listen to His words and live by them. As they remember their identity as sons and daughters who are a treasured possession and a kingdom of priests, rather than grumble about the chaos of the circumstances in which they find themselves, they will see God's will accomplished in all manner of ways. It will even include young boys being delivered from debilitating demons. They are to set their eyes on the revelation of Sinai and the worship of God instead of giving in to their fears as Israel did in the wilderness. If they do the former, they will know their calling and exercise mustard-seed faith.

> As they remember their identity as sons and daughters who are a treasured possession and a kingdom of priests, rather than grumble about the chaos of the circumstances in which they find themselves, they will see God's will accomplished in all manner of ways.

Thus, "the mountain that will be moved from here to there" does not represent the circumstances or problems we face in our individual lives, even though it is often interpreted this way. This mountain represents Sinai, the place where by giving the law and the commandments,

God made known His will for His son Israel to be a people of worship. Again, when we place our eyes on the mountain rather than our circumstances, obey His word, and engage in worship, then we will see the impossible accomplished. It will be like the deliverance of Israel from Egypt, and we will experience freedom for worship in our own lives.

Moses came down from Sinai to meet a fearful and confused people who had made an image of an Egyptian god in hopes of being saved from the God of thunder and fire on the mountain. In the same way, Jesus comes down from His own Sinai, His own place of revelation and affirmation of God's covenantal purpose, to find His disciples unable to deliver a boy from being cast into the fire. Just as Moses was angry because the people recoiled from God and instead worshipped an idol that Aaron said magically leaped out of a kiln, so also Jesus is upset because the disciples cannot bring deliverance to a boy who keeps getting thrown into the fire and water. Rather than manifest faith born out of relationship with God, the disciples show little faith and become hypnotized by the problem. This is not the way of Sinai; it is not the way of mustard-seed faith.

SINAI THEOLOGY

According to Matthew, much of Jesus' ministry figuratively occurs on Mt. Sinai. On the mountain of temptation, He commits Himself to God's will, and on the mountain of ascension, He bequeaths power upon His followers for the purification and worship of the nations. And it is on yet another mountain that Jesus is transfigured like Moses and teaches the disciples that they are to be people of mustard-seed faith, by which He means men and women who hear God's word and live according to its revelation despite the cares and storms of life. Such men and women will see God's deliverance power exercised through them as He sets people free to worship Him.

It is easy to focus our attention on the problems we face and become misled or distracted from our course in life. When we focus on our circumstances, we cannot see the way God has set before us. We cannot see what He is doing, and we cannot hear His voice. We cultivate a "little faith" mindset. We become distracted, and distraction leads to unbelief. Like the disciples, we say to God, "Don't you care?" Whether it be our need for food and clothes, the storms of life that batter against us, or the distraction of real circumstances that keep us from remembering what God has said, we show ourselves to be like ancient Israel in the wilderness when we see these things as the exclusive determining factors in our lives. The answer is mustard-seed faith that holds to God's Sinai word during such times and experiences the transformation that such a tenacious hold brings.

Reflection and Discussion

1. What clues does Matthew give to his readers that the mountain of transfiguration is a symbol of Mt. Sinai?
2. What is mustard-seed faith?
3. Can you think of times in your life when you have responded with "little faith"? Can you name times when you have responded with "mustard-seed faith"?

7

Jesus' Sinai Sermon

ACCORDING TO MATTHEW, Jesus delivers a Sinai message to His disciples when He goes "up on the mountain."[1] The importance of the message is evident in the threefold way Matthew introduces it: "And he opened his mouth and taught them, saying" (Matthew 5:2). Jesus opens His mouth, He teaches the people, and He speaks. The words that follow are spoken by One who is a new and greater Moses, whose teaching on the mountain favorably compares to the Torah that God gave at Mt. Sinai.

The sermon is tied together by the theme of righteousness, which Matthew shows to be the practical expression of covenant relationship with God in the life of Jesus' followers. Jesus begins by describing His followers as blessed people who are to bless others as salt and light. He then discusses the nature of righteousness and comments

---

1. In addition to this mountain and those of temptation, transfiguration, and ascension, Matthew places Jesus on the Mount of Olives three times—when He enters Jerusalem prior to His passion; when He talks about the end of the age the week of Passover; and when He goes to Gethsemane after the Last Supper. By linking these events to the Mount of Olives, Matthew identifies Jesus as Messiah, since tradition and Scripture anticipated the appearance of the Messiah at that place.

on specific Torah commands. Jesus follows this teaching with a model prayer for His disciples, elaborating on what the prayer means in terms of faith and forgiveness. He concludes His message with an exhortation to act upon His words that are the rock upon which they are to build their lives (Matthew 5–7).

THE BEATITUDES (MATTHEW 5:3–12)

Jesus begins His sermon by describing blessed people. Rather than turning to health, wealth, and knowledge as signs of blessing, He points instead to sorrow, meekness, righteousness, mercy, purity, and peace. He says that blessing may be found even in persecution. By displaying these qualities in their lives, His disciples will show they are related to Him and prepared to receive the rewards, including a place in God's kingdom, comfort, inheritance, righteousness, mercy, vision, and acceptance as God's sons and daughters. A closer look reveals that *these rewards resemble God's blessings to Israel in the Exodus.* For example, God makes His will (kingdom) known to Israel in His commandments and instructions for worship. He comforts them in their tribulation through His personal presence. He gives them an inheritance of a land of milk and honey. He reveals a way of righteousness in the Torah. He shows mercy at the Red Sea and in the wilderness. He shows His back (a vision of Himself) to Moses on the mountain. He calls Israel His son. Truly blessed people are like the Israelites who have received His word, know

His will, and have experienced His personal presence
and abundant provision. Such people reflect the very life
of God, who in the Exodus became poor for His people
and shared in their suffering; who humbled Himself and
abided with them; who showed Himself to be righteous,
merciful, and pure in all His ways with them; who made
peace with His difficult and hard-hearted people; and who
bore the grumbling and complaining of His people with
understanding.

Matthew arranges the beatitudes in the form of a
Hebrew chiastic poem—a literary type in which each line
of the poem has a matching line and the two lines in the
middle represent the poem's primary point. At the heart of
this chiasm are the primary characteristics of the followers
of Jesus.

Poor in Spirit

Mournful

The meek

Those who hunger and thirst for righteousness

The merciful

Pure in heart

Peacemakers

Those who are persecuted and
reviled for righteousness

The two attributes at the heart of the Beatitudes are
righteousness and mercy. The word *mercy* translates the
Greek *eleos*, which likely translates the Hebrew *hesed*. It
describes *the primary attribute that God displayed when
He delivered Israel from Egypt.* This attribute is seen when

He passes by Moses on the mountain and proclaims His name, saying, "The Lord, the Lord, a God merciful and gracious, slow to anger, and abounding in steadfast love (*hesed*) and faithfulness, keeping steadfast love (*hesed*) for thousands." (Exodus 34:6–7).[2] Prior to this, Moses sings of God's mercy at the parting of the Red Sea: "You have led in your steadfast love (*hesed*) the people whom you have redeemed" (Exodus 15:13). And when the prophet Isaiah recalls the story of the Exodus, he begins by referring to God's mercy: "I will recount the *steadfast love* (*hesed*) of the Lord (Isaiah 63:7). From beginning to end, the Exodus story is one of God's mercy.

The disciples are blessed when they imitate God by showing mercy to others, just as the Lord showed Himself to be merciful and long-loving at Sinai. Matthew especially shows Jesus as merciful and ministering *hesed*. Time after time, people approach Him and ask for mercy. A Canaanite woman wants mercy for her daughter who is possessed by a demon. A father wants mercy for his son who is plagued by seizures. Two blind men want mercy from the son of David and have their sight restored (Matthew 15:21–28; 17:14–18; 20:29–34). None of these people have any claim on Jesus, of course. None of them say they are deserving of His favor. All of them resemble the people of Israel who needed deliverance from their bondage and blindness in Egypt. In fact, Matthew shows that they are aware they are asking for something that they can't barter or buy, but

---

2. The words *merciful* and *steadfast love* in these verses are *rahûm* and *hesed* in Hebrew and translated *eleos* and *polueleos* in the Greek Septuagint.

they ask anyway because Jesus comes into their presence and makes Himself available to them. Not unlike God who made Himself available to Israel by leading them out of Egypt and then establishing a covenant with them, Jesus goes among the people to lead them out of their own places of servitude and bondage.

Those who hunger and thirst for righteousness are people who want a relationship with God based on His *hesed*. Psalm 107 describes the exiled people as hungry and thirsty. They are filled with "good things" because of God's mercy. The psalmist exhorts: "Oh give thanks to the Lord, for he is good, for his steadfast love (*hesed*) endures forever!" The people give thanks because God has delivered them from east and west, north and south. They sing:

> Some wandered in desert wastes,
>> finding no way to a city to dwell in;
> hungry and thirsty,
>> their soul fainted within them.
> Then they cried to the Lord in their trouble,
>> and he delivered them from their distress.
> He led them by a straight way
>> till they reached a city to dwell in.
> Let them thank the Lord for his steadfast love [*hesed*],
>> for his wondrous works to the children of man!
> For he satisfies the longing soul,
>> and the hungry soul he fills with good things
>> (Psalm 107:4–9).

> Those who hunger and thirst for righteousness are people who want a relationship with God based on His *hesed.*

Jesus recalls this psalm when He tells His disciples that those who hunger for relationship with God will be satisfied. When people want to be restored in their lives to God, God will provide for them and show them mercy.

Here at the heart of the Beatitudes is nothing other than the greatest commandment given at Sinai. One day when asked by a scribe to name the most important of God's commandments, Jesus replied:

> "You shall love the Lord your God with all your heart and with all your soul and with all your mind. This is the great and first commandment. And a second is like it: You shall love your neighbor as yourself. On these two commandments depend all the Law and the Prophets" (Matthew 22:36–40).

To love God and to love one's neighbor is equivalent to hungering for righteousness on the one hand and showing mercy on the other. As noted earlier, to hunger for righteousness is desperately to want a relationship with God. This connection can only happen when we love Him with all of our life. Similarly, to show mercy is to love our neighbor as ourselves, because we give to them what God has given to us. To those who want to know God and love Him, God will make Himself known to them. This is the "great and first commandment."

SALT AND LIGHT (MATTHEW 5:13–16)

Jesus follows His description of Sinai character traits with remarks on His mission for His followers. They are to be salt and light throughout the whole earth. Jesus already promised the meek would inherit the earth, recalling Psalm 37, where the psalmist shows that meekness is waiting on the Lord by giving preference to His word and by worshipping Him. Those who do these things will inherit the land God has prepared for them. The Greek wording here, *tē gē*, can be translated as "the earth" or "the land." Jesus draws the disciples' attention to Israel's calling with these words and announces that they are salt and light in the same way that Israel was to be salt and light to the nations. Their mission is an extension of Israel's original calling. As these disciples live by the word that God gives them through Jesus and faithfully worship Him, they will live in a way that reflects Israel's life.

This is a great responsibility. Jesus recalls Israel's experience when He says salt that has lost its saltiness "is no longer good for anything except to be thrown out and trampled under people's feet" (Matthew 5:13). Sadly, this very thing happened at the hands of the Assyrians in the 8th century and the Babylonians in the 7th and 6th centuries. Jesus says that when Israel became like other nations, she was thrown out into exile and subjected to the ways and laws of those nations. Israel was trampled under the feet of the people of Assyria and Babylon and was no longer good for anything because her witness to God's word through her worship was diminished in her ambition to be like those nations.

Jesus' disciples are also to be light in the same way the people of Israel were to be the light of the world—they were to be the lamp of God's household and shine so that all people everywhere would behold God's glory in their worship. Isaiah had this vision when he prophesied that God's servant, which many at the time saw as an allusion to the whole people, would be light to the nations. God declares through the prophet:

> Behold my servant, whom I uphold,
>> my chosen, in whom my soul delights;
> I have put my Spirit upon him;
>> he will bring forth justice to the nations....
> He will not grow faint or be discouraged
>> till he has established justice in the earth;
>> and the coastlands wait for his law....
>
> I will give you as a covenant for the people,
>> a light for the nations,
>> to open eyes that are blind,
> to bring out the prisoners from the dungeon,
>> from the prison those who sit in darkness.
> I am the Lord; that is my name;
>> my glory I give to no other (Isaiah 42:1–8).

This vision is also in Jesus' mind when He tells the disciples that they are to be light. They are to continue to exercise the privilege given to Israel and Moses at Sinai. They are to be a priesthood of God's glory and

shine forth God's marvelous light to the nations
in worship.

Jesus' disciples are also to
be light in the same way the
people of Israel were to be the light
of the world—they were to be the
lamp of God's household and shine
so that all people everywhere would
behold God's glory in their worship.

JESUS AND THE COMMANDMENTS
(MATTHEW 5:17–48)

To be salt and light in the world requires a greater
righteousness than that exemplified by the Pharisees.
Jesus' declaration would have daunted his disciples. After
all, the Pharisees demonstrated great righteousness in
their precise devotion to the Torah and the traditions that
had developed in response to it. Nonetheless, the nature
of their mission is outlined in the Law and the Prophets,
which Jesus says He has come to fulfill. He has not come
to set the Law and Prophets aside; rather, He came to see
that they are upheld. So, what does he mean by greater
righteousness? What He doesn't mean is that His followers
should develop their own newer and better traditions.
In fact, Jesus later warns them about the "leaven of the
Pharisees," which refers to the expansion of God's law, like
leaven in dough, in their many interpretations of the law.
In Jesus' mind, exceeding righteousness emphasizes the

intent of God's word in the commandments rather than the incremental interpretation of that word, though helpful and needful as such may be. Jesus wants the relationship His followers have with His Father to be grounded in the Father's will as expressed in His word rather than human opinion as found in the traditions.

Jesus gives several examples of this principle from the commandments God gave Moses at Sinai. The first involves murder:

> "You have heard that it was said to those of old,
> 'You shall not murder; and whoever murders
> will be liable to judgment.' But I say to you that
> everyone who is angry with his brother will be liable
> to judgment; whoever insults his brother will be
> liable to the council; and whoever says, 'You fool!'
> will be liable to the hell of fire. So if you are offering
> your gift at the altar and there remember that your
> brother has something against you, leave your gift
> there before the altar and go. First be reconciled
> to your brother, and then come and offer your gift"
> (Matthew 5:21–24).

Jesus interprets the commandment to show that murder is nothing other than the extreme form or unrestrained expression of the attitude of anger. If unchecked, anger ultimately manifests itself in murder. So when a man gives a peace offering to the Lord as prescribed in the law, he should first make peace with anyone with whom he is angry. He should deal with the attitude of his heart so that he can come before God free of confusion and conflict (Leviticus 3). This is the type of greater righteousness to which Jesus refers. In Jesus' mind, the commandment against murder is not about a violent act alone but also what such an act represents—unfettered anger.

Very likely, Jesus was considering the story of Cain and Abel at this point in His sermon (Genesis 4:1–12). Cain allowed his anger—the attribute or sin that was crouching at the door of his heart—to act without restraint against his brother when God rejected Cain's offering and accepted Abel's. His anger was the problem, and the murder of his brother was the brutal expression of it.[3] According to Jesus, any type of activity or speech, such as insults and name-calling that harms or demeans another person is but a less violent form of the attitude of anger which, in its purest expression, shows itself in murder. This is what Jesus means when He exhorts His disciples to cultivate greater righteousness in their lives. Greater or exceeding righteousness gives attention to motivation, which is related to one's heart.

> According to Jesus, any type of activity or speech, such as insults and name-calling that harms or demeans another person is but a less violent form of the attitude of anger which, in its purest expression, shows itself in murder.

---

3. In the story, Cain becomes angry when God rejects his offering of grain but accepts the firstborn of Abel's flock of sheep. When Jesus says a person should be reconciled to a brother before giving a gift to God at the temple, He infers that Cain already held a grudge against Abel before acting upon it and murdering him.

Jesus gives several additional examples of exceeding righteousness in relation to the commands of Sinai and concludes with an exhortation for His followers to love their enemies and to "be perfect, as your heavenly Father is perfect." The love of neighbors at that time was enlightened thinking, but the love of enemies was unthinkable. Yet, Jesus' disciples are to exceed what others desire or demand from them. This is why Jesus speaks of turning the other cheek, giving away one's tunic, or going two miles instead of one. He is not encouraging His followers to suffer indiscriminate abuse. Rather, He is encouraging them to show *a righteousness that does not give as good as it gets but gives better* than what the law allows or circumstances justify. The law permitted punishment, restitution, and reparation. It permitted the slap of a hand, the taking of a tunic, and forced labor. Jesus commands His disciples to show the perfection of God their Father, which is exceeding righteousness, and they are to imitate Him. And what kind of righteousness did God show to the disciples' ancestors? As seen previously, Israel's God had experienced the same servitude as His people in Egypt. He *knew* their suffering because He shared in it in some mysterious way. He *knew* what it was like to be slapped around and have tunics taken away in Egypt. And He also went with them into the wilderness and remained with them even after they refused to enter the Promised Land. He wandered in the wilderness with His people for an additional 38 years. He went two miles instead of one. God Himself modeled exceeding righteousness in the Exodus.

To be perfect like God does not mean that Jesus' followers should expect to live sinless lives. It is to live in such a way to reflect God's ways to others as His image to them. It is to act toward others in love in the same way God acted toward ancient Israel. Such divine love is righteous and full of mercy, like that manifested in the Exodus at Mt. Sinai.

JESUS' EXODUS PRAYER (MATTHEW 6:5–7:27)

The remainder of Jesus' sermon highlights the prayer that His disciples will pray and His elaboration on its meaning:

> "Our Father in heaven,
> hallowed be your name.
> Your kingdom come,
> your will be done,
> on earth as it is in heaven.
> Give us this day our daily bread,
> and forgive us our debts,
> as we also have forgiven our debtors.
> And lead us not into temptation,
> but deliver us from evil" (Matthew 6:9–13).

To pray this prayer is to pray the Exodus story. The disciples are to begin by addressing God as Father. They are to relate to Him in the same way as the Israelites, who knew God as Father and were called His sons in the Exodus from Egypt (Exodus 4:22; 3:14). They also are to declare His name to be holy in how they live, just as the Israelites were to be holy like God by keeping His commandments. Moreover, Jesus' disciples are to ask for the kingdom of God to come and His purposes to be performed in their lives. Since it is impossible to do the work of the kingdom or perform His will without His help, they are to ask for "daily bread," which is the provision they need so that they can do what He wants. The request for bread recalls the manna God gave the Israelites in the wilderness each day to sustain them in their journey. The manna was what they needed as they learned God's law and way of worship and how they were to live as His people according to His will expressed in the law.

They are then to ask for and to offer forgiveness. All of the Levitical law that God gave Moses on Sinai prescribed the sacrificial ritual that the people were to practice in their relationship with Him. The entire system was a form of worship showing them how they were to receive God's forgiveness and forgive one another.

The disciples will experience times in the wilderness like the Israelites and even like Jesus at the beginning of His ministry. "Lead us not into temptation" does not suggest that God tempts His people but instead affirms that He works in their lives for deliverance. The statement means: "You don't lead us into temptation, but You deliver us from evil!" The disciples are to pray that God will sustain them with provision as He delivers them from evil. Their ancestors succumbed to temptation and decried God's ways even though He had set them free from the evil of slavery and the false gods of Egypt. They grew tired of the manna and wanted the leeks of Egypt;

they feared the fire on the mountain and built a golden calf; they tasted the grapes of Canaan but thought only about the giants in the land. And time after time, they accused Moses and the Lord of leading them into the wilderness to be killed. They did not see their journey out of Egypt as divine deliverance but rather as a trial and temptation. The disciples are to remind themselves in prayer that the trials and temptations they will face are common to the struggles that follow deliverance from darkness. They are to follow the example of Jesus Himself who resisted the temptation of the evil one in the wilderness by recalling the words of Sinai and committing to their obedience and the way of worship.[4]

> "Lead us not into temptation" does not suggest that God tempts His people but instead affirms that He works in their lives for deliverance.

Praying this prayer would have reminded the disciples of the Israelites and the Exodus and challenged them to live out that story in their own life together. It would have affirmed that they were a new generation called to worship God and show His glory to the nations.

---

4. Jesus says to the devil, according to Matthew, "Man shall not live by bread alone, but by every word that comes from the mouth of God" (Matthew 4:4). He quotes from Deuteronomy 8:3 in doing so and recalls the words spoken by God to Moses on the mountain.

THE ROCK OF REVELATION

Jesus concludes His Sinai sermon with an exhortation to His disciples to build their lives on the rock of the words He has given to them. He says,

> "Everyone then who hears these words of mine and does them will be like a **wise man** who built his house on the rock. And the rain fell, and the floods came, and the winds blew and beat on that house, but it did not fall, because it had been founded on the rock" (Matthew 7:24–25).

Later Jesus says to the disciples that He will build His church on "this rock" and "the gates of hell shall not prevail against it" (Matthew 16:18). He says this in response to Peter's declaration that He is "the Christ, the Son of the Living God." Peter's words are not his own, Jesus says. They are revelation from the Father: "Blessed are you, Simon bar-Jonah! For flesh and blood has not revealed this to you, but my Father who is in heaven" (Matthew 16:17). Peter's declaration is nothing less than a divine revelation of Jesus' identity. Jesus' enthusiastic response is due to the fact that it is the same revelation He Himself was given when He was baptized at the Jordan River and heard the voice from heaven say, "This is my beloved Son, with whom I am well pleased" (Matthew 3:17). The revelation He received then has reached one of His disciples now. The rock upon which Jesus will build His church is the same rock upon which He resisted the temptation of the devil and built His ministry. It is the revelatory rock of God's word that is the

unshakeable foundation for all human life and the firm
footing for the disciples' lives.

> The rock upon which Jesus
> will build His church is the
> same rock upon which He resisted
> the temptation of the devil and built
> His ministry.

This revelatory rock of God's word was first experienced
by the Israelites in the wilderness at Mt. Sinai. There, God
spoke the Ten Words in thunder and fire to Moses and the
people. The words were revelation to the people for the
foundation of their life together. Israel was the original
"wise man" to whom Jesus refers in the sermon parable,
who had been given the words of God to live by on the rock
of Sinai.

Because of God's commandments, the nations would
wonder at the wisdom of Israel. Thus, Moses exhorted the
people to obey them:

"See, I have taught you statutes and rules, as the
Lord God commanded me, that you should do them
in the land that you are entering to take possession
of it. Keep them and do them, for that will be **your
wisdom** and your understanding in the sight of
the peoples, who, when they hear all these statutes,
will say, 'Surely **this great nation is a wise** and
understanding people.' For what great nation is
there that has a god so near to it as the Lord our
God is to us, whenever we call upon him? And what
great nation is there, that has statutes and rules so

righteous as all this law that I set before you today?"
(Deuteronomy 4:5–8).

In this passage, the commandments God gave Israel at
the rock of Sinai were to be a testimony to the nations of
His wisdom in them. They would be a wise people as long
as they lived by His revelatory words. Jesus' disciples will
show themselves to be the wise sons and daughters like
those Israelites when they live by God's words given to
them through the new and greater Moses on the mountain.

SINAI THEOLOGY

Jesus' Sinai sermon is about the exceeding righteousness
God desires from His people. It is about a righteousness
that is centered in His *hesed* and reaches out to the whole
earth. God wants His people to inherit the earth and lead
it in worldwide worship as salt and light. It is the very
same righteousness that God wanted to cultivate in the life
of the Israelites when He led them out of Egypt to Sinai
and gave them an example of how to live as a kingdom of
priests in His word full of wisdom and truth.

Jesus calls us to shape our lives upon the words He
teaches and the wisdom they contain. He calls us to build
upon the mercy of God and to bring deliverance to others.
He calls us to live by the truths of God's word and not by
human-constructed technicalities. He calls us to pray as
Exodus people who know God as a Father who provides all
we need to please Him and who does not lead us into
temptation. Most of all, He calls us to live on the rock of

revelation that He has given in His own life—He calls us to climb high and live on Sinai, where we can firmly stand against whatever storms may blow our way.

Jesus calls us to shape our lives upon the words He teaches.

Reflection and Discussion

1. In the Beatitudes, Jesus promised rewards to His disciples. What do the rewards resemble?
2. How is hungering after righteousness related to being merciful?
3. Jesus told His disciples to build their lives on a rock. What is this rock?

8

Garments of Glory

AT THE CONCLUSION to his Gospel, Luke recounts Jesus' final words before His ascension: "Thus it is written, that the Christ should suffer and on the third day rise from the dead, and that repentance for the forgiveness of sins should be proclaimed in his name to all nations." Jesus then says that He will send the "promise of the Father" to help His followers make this proclamation. "But stay in the city until you are clothed with power from on high" (Luke 24:46–49). This is Luke's version of the Great Commission, and in it Jesus tells the disciples to go to all nations clothed with power to proclaim forgiveness of sins. They are to participate in the promise of God for Israel to be "a kingdom of priests and a holy nation" (Exodus 19:6). They are to go in the power of Sinai.

THE MINISTRY OF FORGIVENESS

Jesus says the disciples will be clothed (*enduō*) with power (*dunamis*) as they wait in Jerusalem. He uses this language to emphasize the priestly responsibility and authority they will possess. The verb *enduō* is frequently used in the Septuagint to describe the consecration of Aaron and his sons to the priesthood. After the commandments were given to Moses on the mountain, the covenant confirmed, and the tabernacle constructed, then the priests' garments were made. They were garments "for glory and for beauty," made by those with "a spirit of skill," and included the ephod, breastpiece, robe, sash, and turban (Exodus 28:2–3). God instructed Moses, "You shall put them on Aaron your brother, and on his sons with him, and shall anoint them and ordain them and consecrate them, that they may serve me as priests" (Exodus 28:41).[1]

The priests of Israel served as intermediaries between God and His people. Their tasks involved various duties, the most important being the giving of offerings and sacrifices to God so that the people might experience forgiveness for their sins. Forgiveness stood at the very heart of the priesthood's ministry, so it is this ministry that Jesus promises to extend to His disciples at His ascension. Jesus gives His disciples the same power of forgiveness that He Himself possessed during His ministry. It is power that belongs exclusively to God. In fact, it is Jesus' claim to possess power to forgive that alienated so many religious people against Him and caused them to plot His death. Mark gives an example of this when he reports the story of four men who carry

---

1. The details of this service are given in the Book of Leviticus, where we are told that Moses washed them, put the garments on them, and poured oil over them (Leviticus 8:5–13).

their paralyzed friend to Jesus for healing (Mark 2:1–12). Because of the large crowd around Him, the men climb to the roof and lower the man in front of Jesus. Upon seeing this demonstration of faith, Jesus says, "Son, your sins are forgiven." The scribes recoil at this claim because they know that only God possesses such authority. They murmur, "Why does this man speak like that? He is blaspheming! Who can forgive sins but God alone?" Jesus then heals the man to show that He indeed possesses God's right to forgive. According to Mark, Jesus has the right to forgive because He possesses God's Spirit, which, in Luke's words, is to say He is clothed with power.[2]

The centrality of forgiveness in the ministry of Jesus appears in the prayer He teaches the disciples to pray (Matthew 6:9–13). As seen above, Jesus' disciples are to call God their Father and honor His holiness. They are to invoke the Father's will and kingdom and to ask that God give them all they need to fulfill His will. They are then to ask for forgiveness and commit to the forgiveness of others, even as they ask God to protect them from their inclination to temptation and evil. According to this prayer, Jesus teaches the disciples that the essence of life in God's kingdom involves forgiveness and the relationship it establishes with God and other people.

---

2. This does not mean that Mark did not believe in Jesus' divinity. It simply notes a primary emphasis in his Gospel that Jesus possesses the Spirit and, as a result, experiences conflict and resistance throughout His ministry.

According to this prayer, Jesus teaches the disciples that the essence of life in God's kingdom involves forgiveness and the relationship it establishes with God and other people.

In Luke's Gospel, Jesus follows this prayer with a promise about asking and receiving (Luke 11:5–13). A man will get up in the middle of the night to fulfill a neighbor's request, Jesus says, if the neighbor is persistent. Thus, the disciples are to ask, seek, and knock. When they do these things, they will receive: "For everyone who asks receives, and the one who seeks finds, and to the one who knocks it will be opened." Jesus concludes by saying, "How much more will the heavenly Father give the Holy Spirit to those who ask him!" Jesus says that when His disciples pray for (1) God's will to be done, (2) provision to accomplish His will, and (3) forgiveness as the means to live according to that will, they can ask what they desire and expect to receive it. Why is this so? Because they will be asking for the very thing God wants to do—to fulfill His will in them. This is accomplished through the ministry of the Spirit, which is why Jesus promises the Holy Spirit of God the Father. When His disciples pray for forgiveness, they can expect God to send His Spirit to help them give and receive forgiveness in life with one another. They can expect the Spirit to come and give them the priestly ministry of forgiveness.

When His disciples pray for forgiveness, they can expect God to send His Spirit to help them give and receive forgiveness in life with one another.

Forgiveness is the final thing on Jesus' mind during His crucifixion and the first thing on His mind the day of His resurrection. Forgiveness surrounds the death and resurrection of Jesus and binds the two events together. Luke reports that as Jesus hung on a cross between two criminals, He asked His Father to forgive the people who had held Him up to mockery and ridicule.

> Two others, who were criminals, were led away to be put to death with him. And when they came to the place that is called The Skull, there they crucified him, and the criminals, one on his right and one on his left. And Jesus said, "Father, forgive them, for they know not what they do" (Luke 23:32–34).

Here, in the midst of His personal dissolution, Jesus speaks words of forgiveness. With His last breath, Jesus thinks of the men who are pouring out their anger, lust, and fear upon Him, rather than thinking of His own need for deliverance.

Forgiveness remains on Jesus' mind the morning of His resurrection. According to John, after Jesus appears to Mary, He then goes to the disciples with words of peace. He breathes on them and says, "Receive the Holy Spirit. If you forgive the sins of any, they are forgiven; if you withhold

forgiveness from any, it is withheld" (John 20:22–23).
Here John highlights a central feature of the worship that
the newly formed priesthood of disciples will offer to God.
It is worship in Spirit and truth. It issues from God's people
who have asked for and received discerning forgiveness
from one another through the help of the Holy Spirit. This
worship that they offer with the help of the Holy Spirit is
given in unity by people who have been reconciled to one
another. By breathing on His disciples, Jesus clothes them
with the Spirit to serve as priests through the proclamation of repentance and forgiveness of sins.

This clothing in power is completed when the Spirit
moves in the form of fire upon the disciples on the Day of
Pentecost. Just as Moses and Israel stood near to the fire on
the mountain to be empowered with the law and reconciled
to God and one another through the covenant it represented,
so also Jesus' disciples are clothed with the Spirit to exercise
forgiveness with one another. This is why Peter concludes
his Pentecost-day message after the Spirit has moved upon
the disciples by saying to those who have gathered, "Repent
and be baptized every one of you in the name of Jesus Christ
for the forgiveness of your sins, and you will receive the gift
of the Holy Spirit" (Acts 2:38). In addition to exercising the
priestly ministry of forgiveness at this time, Peter urges
those who hear his words to receive the gift of the Spirit so
that they may exercise such ministry themselves.

Finally, when prior to His ascension Jesus says the
disciples will be clothed with power, He connects their
empowerment with His own ministry. According to Luke,
it was in a synagogue in Nazareth, after returning from the

wilderness, that Jesus read from Isaiah 61 about the Lord's servant who has the Spirit to proclaim freedom, favor, and judgment to the nations. The passage goes on to say that God will give His people a beautiful turban and garment of praise and call them His priests. It also says,

> "Strangers shall stand and tend your flocks; foreigners shall be your plowmen and vinedressers; but you shall be called the priests of the Lord; they shall speak of you as the ministers of our God; you shall eat the wealth of the nations, and in their glory you shall boast" (Isaiah 61:5–6).

The passage concludes with the servant saying that "[the Lord] has clothed me with the garments of salvation; he has covered me with the robe of righteousness" (Isaiah 61:10). The entire passage from Isaiah that Jesus reads in the synagogue describes the ministry of God's servant who will deliver the nations and return the priesthood to God's people. The nations will bless the people of Israel by tending their flocks and plowing their fields as Israel fulfills her priestly responsibilities toward them. Though Jesus only reads the first couple of verses of this passage in Isaiah, all of it would have been on His mind when He said that Isaiah's words were now fulfilled in Him. By promising to clothe the disciples with power at His ascension, Jesus means that they will enjoy the same priestly authority that He, as the Spirit-anointed Servant of Lord, has exercised among them from the beginning of His ministry. It is the authority to bring deliverance to all people through forgiveness and to lead in the way of worship.

CLOTHED WITH GLORY

This ministry of forgiveness is for reconciliation, and it reprises Adam's privilege in the beginning when God declared that he would bear His image and likeness. Adam was created to reflect the presence of the Creator throughout the creation. The transcendent God of all things intended to be immanent to His creation through Adam, whom He made to be His priest over the creation.[3]

As a priest, Adam was not clothed with a robe but with God's own beauty and glory. This is the meaning of his nakedness prior to his disobedience: "The man and his wife were both naked and were not ashamed" (Genesis 2:25). Not to be ashamed means to enjoy honor. They enjoyed honor because they were clothed in God's glory, reflecting His presence, and they remained in this condition until succumbing to the serpent's temptation. The story says they were naked (*ārûmmîm*), but the serpent was crafty (*ārûm*). The Hebrew words are from different roots but sound similar. The author plays with this alliteration to show Adam's natural condition in relation to God in the garden in contrast to his condition under the influence of the serpent. The husband and his wife were clothed in God's glory as they reflected His image in the creation. When Adam broke God's command not to eat the fruit of the Tree of Knowledge, he covered his nakedness (glory) with the

---

3. As noted above, this is evident in the Hebrew words *ābad* and *šāmar*, which are used to describe Adam's responsibilities in the garden. Though the words are translated as *work* and *keep*, they are often used to describe the activities of priests in the tabernacle and temple. Adam is a priest. See my comments in *The Trees Will Clap Hands*, 9–10.

serpent's deception. He became preoccupied with himself and began to act with deceitfulness, similar to the way of the serpent who had tempted him.

God acts to preserve Adam's priestly role in creation by clothing the man and woman with "garments of skins" that, according to John Sailhamer, "anticipates the notion of sacrifice in the slaying of the animals for the making of the skin tunics...."[4] Sacrifice is associated with Adam's new garments. The same Hebrew word is used later when Moses makes garments for Aaron and his sons to wear as priests to cover their nakedness and protect them from death (Exodus 28:40–43). God's act of clothing Adam looks ahead to His preparation of Aaron and his sons to continue the service assigned to Adam in the beginning.[5]

The significance of this original glory in Adam is touched upon by C.S. Lewis in his sermon, "The Weight of Glory." In this World War II message, Lewis comments on human nature and the biblical promise of glory. Of all the promises of Scripture, the one that was hardest for him to understand was this one. Lewis says that such a promise caused him to envision personal fame on the one hand, which seemed self-centered, and luminosity on the other, which seemed ridiculous. Neither of these notions of glory comported with his idea of Christian humility.[6] Yet, upon reflection, Lewis saw that the Bible does not depict the gift of glory as human fame or personal popularity; instead, it equates glory with divine acceptance and approval: "The promise of glory is the

---

4. Sailhamer, *The Pentateuch as Narrative*, 109.
5. Ibid.
6. Lewis, *The Weight of Glory*, 36.

promise, almost incredible and only possible by the work of Christ, that some of us ... shall find approval, shall please God."[7] Biblical glory describes approval with our Creator who is greater than we are and desires to say, "Well done." It is not concerned with our status in relation to one another; rather, it is about divine approval for which we were created in order to reflect praise back to Him.

Neither does the Bible depict glory as bright luminosity, although it is often described in terms of brilliance and radiance. Such language is metaphorical, Lewis says, and conveys the idea of the beauty of glory that we all desire in some way. All of us have a natural appreciation for beauty that draws us to those things we regard as beautiful. Yet, we don't want to simply appreciate beauty, Lewis writes— "We want to be united with the beauty we see, to pass into it, to receive it into ourselves, to bathe in it, to become part of it."[8] Our desire to gaze indefinitely upon a sunset or to listen to a piece of music over and over again are examples, Lewis would say, of our yearning for something greater than we are that is refracted in the picture or conveyed by the music. In the same way, we want to experience glory and share in it. We have been created to add to the beauty of God's creation and participate in His glory.

> We have been created to add to the beauty of God's creation and participate in His glory.

---

7. Ibid., 38–39.
8. Ibid., 42.

The implications of this are as staggering as a climb to the top of Everest or an ascent to the pinnacle of Sinai. To know that we have been created for acceptance by our Creator and invited to participate in His beauty places great responsibility upon us as to how we should live with one another. Lewis writes,

> It is hardly possible to think too often or too deeply about [the glory] of [one's] neighbor. The load, or weight, or burden of my neighbor's glory should be laid on my back, a load so heavy that only humility can carry it, and the backs of the proud will be broken. It is a serious thing to live in a society of possible gods and goddesses, to remember that the dullest and most uninteresting person you can talk to may one day be a creature which, if you saw it now, you would be strongly tempted to worship...."[9]

He continues,

> "There are no *ordinary* people. You have never talked to a mere mortal. Nations, cultures, arts, civilizations—these are mortal, and their life is to ours as the life of a gnat. But it is immortals whom we joke with, work with, marry, snub, and exploit...."[10]

Lewis is prescient. We don't look upon one another as "gods" or "immortals." We don't see the glory in our neighbor or coworker for which they were created. This lack is due in part to the fact that *we don't see the glory for which we were created.* Can it be that we were created to

9. Ibid., 45–46.
10. Ibid., 46 (his italics).

shine as stars in the heavens? Did God design us to reflect His brilliance as the sun in the sky? Have we been endowed with God's Spirit to worship Him in such a way that we hear, "Well done," which can only mean that we have done good like He did in the beginning when He created all things good? (Genesis 1:31) We think such thoughts are proud and arrogant, and so we quickly banish them from our minds. Yet Lewis would say that not making a place for God's desire in our thinking is false humility. It is to conclude that God cannot and never intended to involve His creation in His glory. Lewis would say that true humility is found in experiencing the pleasure of our Creator. When we worship our God by showing obedience to His Word and finding welcome in His presence, we are clothed with His glory to show forth His praises throughout the whole world. We were created to be clothed with the glory of God. To reflect the brilliance of His being is the reason for our existence. The writer of Genesis says that Adam was made *to be* the image and likeness of God over creation.[11]

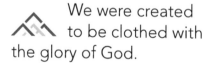

We were created to be clothed with the glory of God.

One way the message of salvation is told in Scripture is through the imagery of clothing. God clothes Adam after

---

11. The Hebrew preposition that is usually translated "in" in Genesis 1:26 ("Let us make man in our image") may also be translated "as" ("Let us make man as [to be] our image").

he eats from the Tree of Knowledge so that Adam might continue to serve Him as a priest. Joseph is given a long multicolored robe by his father as a young man and new clothes by Pharaoh when he is an older, wiser man. The clothing signifies the divine favor he enjoyed at different times in his life. His garments represented God's glory with him to dream dreams and to help lead a nation. David dances without clothing before the Lord to show his humility and dependency upon God for His glory to rule in Israel. Such humility also is manifested when Jesus removes His garments to wash His disciples' feet, and in this way, Jesus shows the original glory of God given to Adam in His ministry to His followers. Paul says that one day all of God's saints will put on new glorious bodies as they worship Him throughout eternity:

> There is one glory of the sun, and another glory of the moon.... So it is with the resurrection of the dead. What is sown is perishable; what is raised is imperishable. It is sown in dishonor; it is raised in glory.... For this perishable body must put on the imperishable, and this mortal body must put on immortality (1 Corinthians 15:41–43, 53).

Jesus' disciples are clothed with power as priests to offer forgiveness to the nations and to reflect glorious praise back to Him so that He will say, "Well done." This fact shows they will be used by God just as He used Adam, Joseph, David, and even His Son Jesus to minister salvation to the world.

THE GLORY OF GOD IN CLAY POTS

Paul expounds upon God's glory in his second letter to the Corinthians: "You show that you are a letter from Christ delivered by us, written not with ink but with the Spirit of the living God, not on tablets of stone but on tablets of human hearts" (2 Corinthians 3:3). What should not be overlooked here is that the ministry of the Spirit in their lives is not unlike the covenant God made with Moses on tablets of stone. The glory given to Moses at Mt. Sinai with the commandments has been extended to the Corinthians. It has come to a people not unlike the generation of Israelites who struggled to live as a covenant community in unity and love when God delivered them out of Egypt. Despite their divisions and disunity, God has chosen to show His glory to them through His Son by the Spirit.

> If [the covenant] came with such glory that the Israelites could not gaze at Moses' face because of its glory,... will not the ministry of the Spirit have even more glory? For if there was glory in the ministry of condemnation, the ministry of righteousness must far exceed it in glory. Indeed, in this case, what once had glory has come to have no glory at all, because of the glory that surpasses it. For if what was being brought to an end came with glory, much more will what is permanent have glory (2 Corinthians 3:7–11).

Here Paul makes the astonishing claim that the divided and contentious Corinthian believers—every bit as thorny as Israel was when God delivered them from Egypt—are people whom God wants to clothe with glory:

Now the Lord is the Spirit, and where the Spirit
of the Lord is there is freedom. And we all, with
unveiled face, beholding the glory of the Lord, are
being transformed into the same image from one
degree of glory to another (2 Corinthians 3:17–18).

Just as Moses looked upon the glory of God when he
received the commandments of the covenant, the
Corinthian believers are privileged to behold "the glory
of the Lord" in the gospel they have received from Paul.
Like Israel's first prophet who reflected God's glory to the
people, they too will reflect the glory of God in their own
lives by worshipping together in freedom and unity.

All of this is the result of God's mercy (*ḥesed*), Paul says,
picking up a primary theme of the Sinai story. God delivered
Israel and made a covenant with them at the mountain so
they could worship Him because of His mercy. Such mercy
guides Paul in his presentation of the gospel that remains
veiled to many because "the god of this world has blinded
the minds of the unbelievers, to keep them from seeing the
light of the gospel of the glory of Christ" (2 Corinthians 4:4).
After all, were it not for such mercy, Paul would have
remained blind to the love of God for all people manifested
in the humble life of His Son Jesus.

Paul describes this ministry of the gospel among the
Corinthians as "treasure in jars of clay" (2 Corinthians 4:7).
He says that God has chosen to give His Word in this way
and reveal His glory through people like the Israelites
and the Corinthians because it highlights His "surpassing
power." What can account for such divine glory manifested

through such people? Is it shown through people like Paul, who are frail and afflicted? Or people who are "always being given over to death for Jesus' sake, so that the life of Jesus also may be manifested in our mortal flesh?" (2 Corinthians 4:11). The only thing that accounts for this is the life of Jesus manifested in Paul and the Corinthians as they lay down their own lives with the help of the Spirit, proclaiming the gospel to others. Though they are being given over to death, Paul says, God "will raise us also with Jesus and bring us into His presence" (2 Corinthians 4:14). Thus, hardship and affliction are preparation for "an eternal weight of glory beyond all comparison" (2 Corinthians 4:17).

Like Moses who struggled with the Israelites and felt the brunt of their grumbling and complaints, Paul has a similar experience with the Corinthians. Yet all his struggles with them are only preparation for God's glory, even as Moses' struggles prepared him for the glory of God on Sinai. Paul groans with the burdens placed on him and yet is unbowed due to the Spirit who is with him.

SINAI THEOLOGY

God called Israel to His priesthood at Sinai. It was there that men from among them were given the privilege of serving as priests as they learned how to serve the nations. These priests were clothed with garments that represented the glory of God and distinguished them for the ministry of forgiveness through offerings and sacrifices. The priests' garments reveal that God's glory shines brightly among

His people when they live in peace and reconciliation with Him and with one another. For this reason, the primary ministry and expression of worship given to the priests and to Israel was that of forgiveness.

Jesus models forgiveness by expressing it from the cross and declaring it on the day of His resurrection. He bequeaths the ministry of forgiveness to His disciples by clothing them with the Spirit. The Spirit makes forgiveness possible by giving power to ask for and to offer forgiveness on the one hand and giving discernment to determine the truthfulness of repentance on the other hand. By breathing on the disciples the day of His resurrection and then sending the Spirit on the day of Pentecost, Jesus endues or clothes them with the priestly ministry of forgiveness that He possessed while among them.

> Jesus models forgiveness by expressing it from the cross and declaring it on the day of His resurrection.

This same priestly ministry has been given even to the fractious Corinthians, revealing that God has given His Spirit for such a holy and precious calling to fallible people who are very much like jars of clay. Thus, it is God's desire to clothe all believers with the glory of His Spirit to have the power to ask forgiveness of others and to forgive them in return. We all have been given the ministry of reconciliation and the high privilege of reflecting God's presence in His world.

Reflection and Discussion

1. What is the primary ministry that God has given to those who are called to be priests?
2. What is the significance of C.S. Lewis' "Weight of Glory" sermon for believers today?
3. What is the treasure that God has given to the Corinthian believers who Paul describes as "jars of clay"?

9

The Day of Pentecost:
Sinai in the Sanctuary

THE BOOK OF ACTS begins with Jesus' disciples gathered together in Jerusalem at His command, waiting for the promise of the Father. As they wait for this promise, they join in the celebration of Pentecost with fellow Jews from around the ancient Near Eastern world. While at worship that day, they hear a loud sound, see fire fall from above, and speak in different languages. Jews "from every nation under heaven" hear them praising God for His mighty works, confirming that the disciples speak in the heart languages of the nations. Originally, the people of Israel praised God at Sinai for the first fruits of the harvest and for the blessings of the commandments. In the mother tongues of the nations, Jesus' disciples join in that praise. It is a sign of God's desire for the praise of many peoples in relation with His one people.

THE LAST DAYS

Peter interprets the loud sound, the fire, and the multilingual praises of the people as the downpour of God's Spirit (Acts 2:38–39). He does so by citing the prophet Joel and proclaiming, "And in the last days it shall be, God declares, that I will pour out my Spirit on all flesh." (Acts 2:17). His message is that the last days have begun. But *these last days are very much like the first days when God brought Israel out of Egypt.* Peter then quotes the remainder of Joel's message:

> "And I will show wonders in the heavens above
>> and signs on the earth below,
>> blood, and fire, and vapor of smoke;
> The sun shall be turned to darkness
>> and the moon to blood,
>> before the day of the Lord comes, the great
>> and magnificent day.
> And it shall come to pass that everyone who
> calls upon the name of the Lord shall be saved"
> (Acts 2:19–21; cf. Joel 2:28–32).

The imagery of Joel's prophecy is replete with allusions to Sinai: the phrase *wonders in the heavens above* recalls the thunder and lightning at the mountain, even as *signs on the earth below* speaks of the plagues, the parting of the waters, and the manna that preceded the mountain. The *fire and vapor of smoke* describe the presence of God at the mountain that darkened the sun and discolored the moon with ashes and soot in the air. And how else would the day God appeared at Sinai be described other than as a *great and magnificent day?* The passage concludes with the promise of salvation through the name of the Lord, which summarizes the purpose of the Exodus: God gave His name (I Am) to Israel so they would know who had saved them from slavery. The day that Joel prophesied when he declared the Lord's message to His people was informed by the day God visited Israel at Mt. Sinai. Joel looked back to that day of fire and smoke to describe what God was going to do yet again among His people. Joel remembered the signs of the Exodus and looked forward to the mountain's second magnificent day when the people would worship their God by name for their deliverance and salvation. This means that when Peter interprets the tongues of fire and the praises of the people on the day of Pentecost by quoting Joel, he is essentially connecting what God is doing in the present with what He had done in the past at Sinai.

> God gave His name (I Am) to Israel so they would know who had saved them from slavery.

DAVID'S PROPHETIC SONG OF PENTECOST

David anticipated these last days in a song (Psalm 68). The great worshipper-king of Israel recalled the deliverance of the Israelites and worship at Sinai and prophesied that they would be reprised in the future. David filled the song with Exodus allusions, beginning with exultation in God's power over His enemies, "God shall arise, his enemies shall be scattered," and praise for Him "who rides through the deserts [and ...] leads out the prisoners to prosperity...." Specifically, David describes God as the *One of Sinai* who led His people as a flock in the wilderness, in the earthquake and storm, refreshing and sustaining them along the way:

> O God, when you went out before your people,
>> when you marched through the wilderness,
> the earth quaked, the heavens poured down
>> rain,
>> before God, **the One of Sinai**,
>> before God, the God of Israel.
> Rain in abundance, O God, you shed abroad;
>> you restored your inheritance as it languished;
> your flock found a dwelling in it;
>> in your goodness, O God, you provided for
>> the needy (Psalm 68:7–10, emphasis added).

The song continues by boasting that God's army is far greater than Pharaoh's—He commands countless thousands of chariots—and He delivered His people so that they might worship Him. The psalmist declares that God's promise to Moses that the people would worship Him on the mountain will be fulfilled when they bring offerings and gifts to Him:

> The chariots of God are twice ten thousand,
>> thousands upon thousands;
>> the Lord is among them; Sinai is now in the
>> sanctuary.

You ascended on high,
> leading a host of captives in your train
> and receiving gifts among men,
even among the rebellious, that the Lord God
may dwell there (Psalm 68:17–18).

With these lines, David describes God's presence as Sinai, making the mountain a symbol of the Lord Himself. The song exults that the God of the Exodus is and will always be present to His people as their deliverer who receives their worship (gifts). "Sinai is now in the sanctuary" means that the God of deliverance and revelation will be present in the praises of His people.

"Sinai is now in the sanctuary" means that the God of deliverance and revelation will be present in the praises of His people.

The second half of David's song repeats what was said at the beginning: God is victorious over His enemies and will be present at the temple just as He was victorious over Pharaoh when He led the Israelites to Sinai. The Lord will once again show His power and receive the gift of worship from the nations as He vowed would happen at Sinai.

The song boasts, "Our God is a God of salvation, and to God, the Lord, belong deliverances from death" (Psalm 68:20). David envisions the day when this God of salvation will be present in the sanctuary among His people at worship: "Your procession is seen, O God, the procession of my God, my King, into the sanctuary" (Psalm 68:24). The people urge God to gather His people and show them the power that He manifested to their fathers: "Summon your power, O God, the power, O God, by which you have worked for us" (Psalm 68:28).

David concludes by prophesying the worship of God by the nations:

> Because of your temple at Jerusalem
>> kings shall bear gifts to you....
> Nobles shall come from Egypt;
>> Cush shall hasten to stretch out her hands
>> to God.
> O kingdoms of the earth, sing to God;
>> sing praises to the Lord....
> Ascribe power to God,
>> whose majesty is over Israel,
>> and whose power is in the skies.
> Awesome is God from his sanctuary;
>> the God of Israel—he is the one who
>> gives power and strength to his people
>> (Psalm 68:29–35).

This song of David praises God for His power to deliver His people from their enemies, just as He rescued Israel from Egypt, and it describes His presence at the temple as Sinai in the sanctuary. In fact, the song three times identifies God with the sanctuary: in the metaphor of Sinai, in majestic procession, and in awesome power (Psalm 68:17, 24, 35). It declares that God will be present to Israel just as He was to the Israelites at Sinai in His power and will receive gifts and praises from them and from the nations on account of the worship given by His people Israel.

The promise of worship and the exercise of power that God extended to Israel when He brought them out of Egypt was a source of inspiration to David for writing this psalm. He remembered God's deliverance and the great mountain and wrote a song to celebrate that event even as he anticipated a new display of God's power for worship at a future temple and a future time.

In Psalm 68, David prophetically describes the manifestation of the Spirit, so it is not surprising that rabbis later recognized this aspect of the psalm and identified it with the Day of Pentecost. As the disciples gathered in Jerusalem on the very day that all the people celebrated the first fruits of the land and the commandments given to Moses on the mountain, they experienced Sinai in the sanctuary.

THE PROMISE OF THE FATHER

On Pentecost, Jews from near and far traveled to Jerusalem to thank God for the blessing of the early barley harvest and for His faithful provision. At the same time, they thanked God for the gift of His law at Mt. Sinai. N.T. Wright observes, "Passover celebrated the exodus from Egypt; Pentecost, the giving of Torah on Sinai; Tabernacles, the wilderness wandering on the way to the Promised Land."[1] The significance of Pentecost cannot be overstated, since it was at Mt. Sinai that God drew near to His people, gave them His law, and waited to receive their worship. He established their identity and vocation at the mountain. Not only was Israel a delivered people, but they were to be a nation of worshippers. They were to be a kingdom of priests. Thus, when the people gathered in Jerusalem to celebrate the first fruits, they thought of Moses, the giving of the law, the establishment of the covenant, and worship. They rejoiced in the material provision God had made for their physical lives in the early harvest as well as His spiritual provision for worship in the commandments, tabernacle, and sacrificial system.

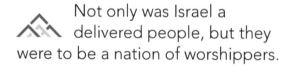

Not only was Israel a delivered people, but they were to be a nation of worshippers.

The Book of Deuteronomy records the details of Pentecost (Deuteronomy 26).[2] The people were to enter the temple with baskets of barley and take them into the court of the priests where they would give praise to God for His faithfulness in leading them into the Promised Land. The priests would take the baskets and place them before

---

1. Wright, *The New Testament and the People of God*, 234. Shmuel Safrai writes, "It may ... be reasonably assumed that the tradition ... saw Pentecost as the festival on which the Torah was given." Safrai and Stern, *The Jewish People in the First Century*, 893.
2. The instructions are given in the future tense since Moses is depicted as giving them to the people while they are in the wilderness.

the altar of the Lord and lead the people in reciting the story of their deliverance from Egypt:

> "A wandering Aramean was my father. And he went down into Egypt and sojourned there, few in number, and there he became a nation, great, mighty, and populous. And the Egyptians treated us harshly and humiliated us and laid on us hard labor. Then we cried to the Lord, the God of our fathers, and the Lord heard our voice and saw our affliction, our toil, and our oppression. And the Lord brought us out of Egypt with a mighty hand and an outstretched arm, with great deeds of terror, with signs and wonders. And he brought us into this place and gave us this land, a land flowing with milk and honey. And behold, now I bring the first of the fruit of the ground, which you, O Lord, have given me" (Deuteronomy 26:5–10).

The offering of the first fruit was an act of gratitude for His mercy and generosity in giving them a land of abundance. It was a response to Moses' exhortation to "rejoice in all the good that the Lord your God has given to you" (Deuteronomy 26:11).

Every third year the people gave a special tithe to Levites and to those in need and, in doing this, showed that they had fulfilled all the commandments that God gave to Moses at Mt. Sinai. They would declare as part of their worship:

> "I have not transgressed any of your command-ments, nor have I forgotten them.... I have obeyed the voice of the Lord my God. I have done according to all that you have commanded me. Look down from

your holy habitation, from heaven, and bless your people Israel and the ground that you have given us, as you swore to our fathers, a land flowing with milk and honey" (Deuteronomy 26:13–15).

In the concluding section of this passage, Moses specifically recalls the giving of the law at Mt. Sinai and exhorts the people continue to live by it.

"This day the Lord your God commands you to do these statutes and rules. You shall therefore be careful to do them with all your heart and with all your soul. You have declared today that the Lord is your God, and that you will walk in his ways, and keep his statutes and his commandments and his rules, and will obey his voice. And the Lord has declared today that you are a people for his treasured possession, as he has promised you, and that you are to keep all his commandments, and that he will set you in praise and in fame and in honor high above all nations that he has made, and that you shall be a people holy to the Lord your God, as he promised" (Deuteronomy 26:16–19).

This is the celebration the disciples join when the Spirit falls upon them in the Book of Acts. Luke's depiction of Pentecost is designed to draw our attention to its similarity with Mt. Sinai in Exodus and Deuteronomy. In the story of the Exodus, the people had journeyed in the wilderness for three months when they arrived at the mountain. There, God spoke to Moses and revealed His purpose for delivering them. He made a covenant with them as His "treasured possession," and as His possession, they would be a "kingdom of priests" and a "holy nation." This meant two things. First, it meant they would share a unique relationship with God as a holy nation, and second, it meant they would serve other peoples as their priesthood.

To prepare for God's arrival in their midst, the people washed themselves and gathered at the base of the mountain where they waited for three days. After this time, God appeared in thunder and fire and spoke to all the people "face to face out of the fire on the mountain," with Moses as the intermediary. The commandments given in fire represent the way of purity by which Israel would honor God and be a witness to the nations. The people were delivered so they could serve God as priests by leading the nations in worship of Him as they lived by the words He gave to them through Moses (Exodus 19).

Likewise, the disciples show their relationship to the Father by obeying Jesus' command and waiting for the promise as the Israelites waited at Sinai. Wind and fire come upon them in a way reminiscent of the thunder and fire on the mountain. The disciples worship God among the nations just as the Israelites were to be a kingdom of priests. The fact that many people from the nations believe in Jesus as a result of the demonstration of worship and Peter's sermon is evidence that the first day of the last days has arrived. Peter and the disciples participate in God's purpose for ancient Israel by leading the nations in worship of God. It is the *first fruits of a universal worship* that all creation will one day give to its Creator (Acts 1–2).

Peter also connects the last days with the promise of the Father, which Jesus described as baptism with the Holy

Spirit. This means that the presence of the Spirit verifies that God has kept His promise. And what is the promise He has kept? It is none other than the one God made to Moses in the wilderness 1,400 years earlier. It is the promise that He would be with Moses and the people to receive their worship on the mountain: "*I will be with you,* and this shall be the sign for you, that I have sent you: when you have brought the people out of Egypt, *you shall serve God on this mountain*" (Exodus 3:12 emphasis added). His desire was that of a Father for His son to gather in His presence, hear His voice, and honor Him. Yet when the people arrived at the mountain and God appeared to them, they trembled, drew away from the fire, and forged a golden idol instead. Now on the Day of Pentecost, God has moved the mountain to the place where Israel, in the form of the followers of Jesus, waits. Pentecost reveals that Mt. Sinai has been uprooted and planted in the midst of God's people Israel—the mountain of revelation and worship has come upon the followers of Jesus—where God is present, His people are called, and they worship Him in freedom. The promise of the Father is the promise God made to Moses to deliver His people so they could worship Him at Sinai as sons and daughters (Exodus 4:22–23). He keeps that promise when by His Spirit He gives Himself to the disciples of Jesus.

Pentecost reveals that Mt. Sinai has been uprooted and planted in the midst of God's people Israel.

THE RIGHT HAND OF THE FATHER

All who have gathered in Jerusalem to celebrate God's great provision in their lives are amazed to hear Galilean men and women speaking their languages, and they say, "We hear them telling in our own tongues the mighty works of God" (Acts 2:11).[3] For what mighty works are the disciples praising God? Certainly, the first thing for which they give praise is the abundant provision He has made for their lives and for the gift of the covenant through the commandments. They praise God for their physical and spiritual lives.

Given the context of the event, they likely praise God for the fulfillment of the promise of the Father. Prior to His ascension, Jesus told the disciples to wait for such a promise. Luke reports, "While staying with them, he ordered them not to depart from Jerusalem, but to wait for the promise of the Father" (Acts 1:4). With the coming of the Spirit, the promise is fulfilled. It is a fulfillment of the words Jesus spoke before His crucifixion that the Father would send a helper (*paraclētos*) to be with the disciples:

"I will ask the Father, and he will give you *another* Helper, to be with you forever ... The helper, the Holy Spirit, whom the Father will send in my name, he will teach you all things ... When the Helper comes, whom I will send

---

3. Luke picks up in the Book of Acts where he left off in his Gospel. Throughout his Gospel, he depicts Jesus as the Savior of all people who is mighty in word and deeds. For people to have seen Him in this way means that they saw Him as a new Moses, used by God to perform acts of power for deliverance. As a result, they saw Jesus as leading a new Exodus.

to you from the Father, the Spirit of truth, who proceeds from the Father ..." (John 14:16, 26; 15:26).

As long as Jesus remained with his disciples, they did not need anyone else to teach them. For forty days after His resurrection, He appeared to them at various times and taught them about the kingdom of God. Luke says, "He presented himself alive after his suffering by many proofs, appearing to them during forty days and speaking about the kingdom of God" (Acts 1:3). After this, He blessed them and "separated" from them.[4] The presence of the Spirit with the disciples on the Day of Pentecost means that another Helper has come to take Jesus' place with them. *The Spirit is the Promise of the Father.*

The presence of the Spirit with the disciples also means that Jesus is with the Father from whom He asks that the Spirit be sent. It means that He is enthroned at the right hand of God. Peter's Pentecost sermon emphasizes this fact. He quotes two psalms of David (Psalm 16 and 110), each of which refers to One who is at God's right hand and concludes: "Being therefore exalted at the right hand of God, and having received from the Father the promise of the Holy Spirit, he has poured out this that you yourselves are seeing and hearing" (Acts 2:33). Several additional New Testament passages describe this as well. For example, when the high priest interrogates Jesus on the night of His passion, he demands to know if Jesus believes He is the Son of God. Jesus says that He does, and "from now on you will

---

4. The Greek word is *diistēmi* and conveys the idea that Jesus will stand away from them.

see the Son of Man seated at the right hand of Power and coming on the clouds of heaven" (Matthew 26:64). "From now on" means that Jesus believes He will soon be enthroned with the Father. Jesus did not envision His installation in authority as a far-distant, abstract eschatological event but a real and imminent one.

> The presence of the Spirit with the disciples also means that Jesus is with the Father from whom He asks that the Spirit be sent. It means that He is enthroned at the right hand of God.

Jesus' installation at the right hand of His Father has occurred by the time Stephen preaches to the high priest and Sanhedrin. His sermon provokes an angry response from these men and concludes with a vision of heaven. At that moment, Stephen declares that he sees Jesus by the throne of heaven: "Behold, I see the heavens opened, and the Son of Man standing at the right hand of God" (Acts 7:56). This event affirms Jesus' prophetic words about Himself before these same men just a short time before (Matthew 26:63–64).

Paul goes further when he writes to the Ephesians and says that God has saved them in His mercy and "seated [them] with [Jesus] in the heavenly places." He makes the bold claim that Jesus' followers sit where He sits in heaven. It is a magnificent and generous gesture that shows "the immeasurable riches of [God's] grace in kindness toward us in Christ Jesus" (Ephesians 2:6–7). In Paul's mind, the Ephesians are seated with God through His Son who has already been installed at the right hand of God's power.

Paul is not the only writer to see Jesus seated next to His Father in heaven. The author of Hebrews begins his sermon by making seven statements about Jesus. The last of these states: "After making purification for sins, [God's Son] sat down at the right hand of the Majesty on high" (Hebrews 1:3). Later, the author declares that Jesus is our high priest who is seated at "the right hand of the throne of the Majesty in heaven" (Hebrews 8:1).

The gift of the Spirit at Pentecost reveals that Jesus is at the right hand of God in heaven, exercising the authority given to Him by His Father. The praises shouted by Jesus' followers for God's mighty works are for the blessing of the first fruits and the gift of God's commandments. They also include the exaltation of God the Father for placing His Son next to Him on the throne. There is no greater work than this. The praises of Pentecost are about the installation of Jesus at the right hand of God, invested with authority, whose first authoritative act is to send another Helper to teach the disciples. The Helper has come to enable these men and women to give worship to God and to lead the nations in worship.

This mighty work of God can only be appreciated in light of His earlier mighty works, the greatest of which Moses says was the deliverance of Israel from Egypt. He marvels at God's power and says that there has been nothing like it before in human history since the creation of Adam.

"For ask now of the days that are past … since the day that God created man on the earth, and ask from one end of heaven to the other, whether such a great thing as this has ever happened or was ever heard of. Did any people ever hear the voice of a god speaking out of the midst of the fire, as you have heard, and still live? Or has any god ever attempted to go and take a nation for himself from the midst of another nation, by trials, by signs, by wonders, and by war, by a mighty hand and an outstretched arm, and by great deeds of terror?" (Deuteronomy 4:32–34).

The answer to Moses' question is a thunderous "No!" There is no equivalent act, since the creation of Adam, to the voice of God out of fire on the mountain. Moses rarely refers to the Exodus and Sinai without describing it as a mighty act. Time and again, he says, "The Lord brought us out of Egypt with a mighty hand. And the Lord showed signs and wonders, great and grievous, against Egypt" (Deuteronomy 6:21–22; 7:18–19; 9:29; 11:2–3).

Peter, too, recalls the power of God in the Exodus when he urges his followers to humble themselves "under the mighty hand of God" so that they may be raised up (1 Peter 5:6). Just as Israel was raised up out of Egypt by God's mighty hand, so too will Peter's audience if they humble themselves and cast their cares upon Him. They are not to worry about the provision that God will make but endure suffering. There can be no doubt that Peter wants his readers to reflect on the plight of the Israelites who, though God raised them with His mighty hand, grumbled at their hardship. They are not to give into such temptations but be restored instead.

When Luke, Paul, and Peter talk about God's great and mighty work in Jesus, their standard for measuring *great* and *mighty* is the power manifested by God in the Exodus in overthrowing Pharaoh and delivering the Israelites. God's great acts refer to the plagues (signs), the parting of the Red Sea, the provision of manna and water from the rock, the voice heard on the mountain in fire, and the tablets written by the finger of God. Luke, Paul, and Peter are thinking of all the wonders of the Exodus, including the voice of God at Sinai, when they write about God's mighty deeds in Jesus.

SINAI THEOLOGY

On the day of Pentecost, Jesus' disciples praise God for His mighty works. With the help of the Spirit who has come upon them, they shout their gratitude for His provision of bread and the commandments. They praise Him for the deliverance of their ancestors and sing the praises of Jesus who is now at the right hand of the Father sending the Spirit. They exult in the enthroned King of Glory. In all of this, they are praising the Father for keeping His promise to Moses and for the mighty work of moving the mountain of revelation and worship into their midst. They are praising Him for fulfilling the prophecy of David's song: "The chariots of God are twice ten thousand, thousands upon thousands; the Lord is among them, Sinai is now in the sanctuary" (Psalm 68:17). They praise God for His presence among them in a special way and for moving the mountain to the temple. On the Day of

Pentecost, Sinai moves to the sanctuary, and the people sing of "the Lord among them" by His Spirit with Jesus at the Father's right hand.

On the Day of Pentecost, Sinai moves to the sanctuary, and the people sing of "the Lord among them" by His Spirit with Jesus at the Father's right hand.

Reflection and Discussion

1. Psalm 68 is a song of David that describes the deliverance of Israel from Egypt. What is its significance for Pentecost?
2. For what are the people praising God on the day of Pentecost?
3. What is the first thing Jesus does when He sits at the right hand of the Father?

10

Paul at Sinai: The Road to Damascus

WHEN PAUL WRITES to the Gentile Christians in Galatia, he gives a brief biographical sketch of his life in support of the gospel he has delivered to them. He recalls his persecution of the church, his zeal for Jewish traditions, and God's calling on him to the Gentiles. He then says that when Jesus appeared to him on the road to Damascus, he did not go to Jerusalem to meet with the apostles but went instead into Arabia (Galatians 1:11–17). It is generally thought that he went into Nabatea (the land south of Damascus and east of the Jordan River) to think about the vision that the Lord had given to him and to make sense of his calling. Where in Nabatea did he go?

PAUL FROM SINAI TO SINAI

Some scholars think that Mt. Sinai is located in Arabia and that Paul imitated Elijah who went to Arabia to be renewed in his faith after the battle with Ahab and Jezebel. N.T. Wright, for example, observes, "Elijah, dejected and depressed, went off to Mount Sinai [in Arabia] to meet his God afresh, to learn about the still small voice as well as the earthquake, wind, and fire. Saul of Tarsus went off, probably to Sinai ... most likely for a similar private wrestling with the God whom he worshipped."[1]

According to this view, Paul followed in the footsteps of the old prophet from Tishbe because he admired him and shared his combative nature. To the Galatians, Paul says:

> For you have heard of my former life in Judaism, how I persecuted the church of God violently and tried to destroy it. And I was advancing in Judaism beyond many of my own age among my people, so extremely zealous was I for the traditions of my fathers (Galatians 1:13–14).

Paul had aggressively persecuted those he thought were leading others astray, much like Elijah, who, full of zeal for Yahweh, defended his God by putting to death hundreds of priests of Baal.[2]

Nonetheless, Elijah is not the only prophet that Paul may have thought about when he went to Mt. Sinai in Arabia. Likely, he intentionally went to the place where he believed Israel's first prophet Moses received the commandments from God. Paul journeyed to the mountain of revelation to think about the vision he had received, to reflect on the word spoken by Ananias that he

---

1. Wright, *Paul for Everyone*, location 210.
2. Paul referred to his persecution of the church several times in his correspondence over the years (Galatians 1:13; Philippians 3:6; 1 Timothy 1:13). See 1 King's 19:10, 14 for a description of Elijah's violent zeal.

was to go to the Gentiles, and to offer worship to the Lord who had shown him such grace. Like Moses, who originally had a vision of God in the burning bush on the mountain and who was said to be the only man to look upon the face of God, Paul had looked upon the glory of the ascended Jesus and was blinded by "a light from heaven [that] flashed around him." He went to the original Sinai to think about his Sinai-like experience on the Road to Damascus.

Paul went to the place where Israel was set apart as a kingdom of priests to lead the nations in the worship of God after hearing Ananias' declaration that he was "a chosen instrument of [God's] to carry [His] name before the Gentiles and kings and the children of Israel" (Acts 9:15). If he were a chosen instrument to take God's name to the Gentiles just as Israel was a chosen people to do the same among the nations, then there was only one place where he must go to pray and to ponder.[3]

PAUL'S SINAI SIGN

No record exists of what Paul experienced on his own Sinai, though it is possible that he gives a glimpse into his experience when he writes about visions and revelations of the Lord and being transported into heaven in his spirit (2 Corinthians 12:1–10). His reference to such a place speaks of being in the immediate presence of God, like

---

3. The Greek word for *chosen* in Acts 9:15 is *eklogēs,* which is related to the word *eklogein* used numerous times in the Exodus story to describe Israel as God's chosen people.

Moses at the summit of Mt. Sinai where he saw God's glory and heard God's name.

> Moses said, "Please show me your glory." And he
> said, "I will make all my goodness pass before you
> and will proclaim before you my name 'The Lord.'
> And I will be gracious to whom I will be gracious, and
> will show mercy on whom I will show mercy. But," he
> said, "you cannot see my face, for man shall not see
> me and live." And the Lord said, "Behold, there is a
> place by me where you shall stand on the rock, and
> while my glory passes by I will put you in the cleft of
> the rock, and I will cover you with my hand until I
> have passed by. Then I will take away my hand, and
> you shall see my back, but my face shall not be seen"
> (Exodus 33:18–23).

Could it be that on the mountain where God revealed His grace and mercy to Israel by making them a kingdom of priests for the nations, Paul understands why he is called to go to those very nations? Was it there that he had confirmed the prophecy Ananias spoke to him? Was it there that God helped him see that He was going to show mercy to the Gentiles as He had done for Israel when He delivered them from Egypt, and that He had selected Paul to carry that message to them?

When Paul describes the revelation and extraordinary experiences that he has received from God, he is conscious of the grace shown to him in those things: "On behalf of this man I will boast, but on my own behalf I will not boast, except of my weaknesses" (2 Corinthians 12:5). Like Moses, who is described as the most humble man to

have ever lived,[4] Paul speaks of his own humility because
the revelation given to him by God and the ministry of
the Spirit in his life were not earned in any way. This is
why he speaks of humility after listing all the struggles,
hardships, and persecutions that he has overcome during
the course of his ministry up to that point. The fact that
Paul had been released from prison, endured beatings,
escaped dangers, and suffered in numerous ways is no
cause for boasting because all those things have been
in service to Jesus who appeared to him in glory. Paul
will boast in the God of Sinai who first showed His
glory to Moses and Israel for the benefit of all the world
(2 Corinthians 11:21–12:6) and who now has revealed
Himself to Paul.

Paul describes a thorn in the flesh related to the revelations he received. Though there are many opinions about
the thorn, it makes sense in the overall span of his ministry
to think of it in terms of his eyesight.[5] When Paul saw
Jesus on the Damascus Road, a light from heaven flashed
around him, and he was blinded. Only later in Damascus,
when Ananias prayed for him, did the scales fall from his
eyes. But was Paul's eyesight perfectly restored? Possibly
not, since it seems that he suffered poor eyesight throughout his ministry. When Paul writes to the Galatians,

---

4. "Moses was very meek (humble), more than all people who were on
the face of the earth" (Numbers 12:3). A couple of verses later, we read
that though God speaks to prophets in visions and dreams, to Moses He
speaks "mouth to mouth, clearly, and not in riddles, and he beholds the
form of the Lord" (Numbers 12:8).

5. The discussion on Paul's eyesight here is adapted from Colin Brown's
Lectures in Systematic Theology at Fuller Theological Seminary.

for instance, he reminds them that they originally met because of an eye infirmity that had disabled him:

> You know it was because of a bodily ailment that I preached the gospel to you at first, and though my condition was a trial to you, you did not scorn or despise me, but received me as an angel of God ... I testify to you that, if possible, you would have gouged out your eyes and given them to me (Galatians 4:13–15).

He closes the same letter by saying, "See with what large letters I am writing to you with my own hand" (Galatians 6:11). One explanation for this remark is that he wrote in large letters because of poor eyesight.

Later, when Paul stands before the Sanhedrin, he denounces one of its members after being slapped in the face for declaring a clear conscience over his teaching. "God is going to strike you, you whitewashed wall!" Paul cries. "Are you sitting to judge me according to the law, and yet contrary to the law you order me to be struck?" When he learns that it was the high priest himself who gave the order, however, he becomes contrite and says that he didn't know and wouldn't have spoken in such an insolent way if he had. How could Paul not have known? The high priest was sitting right before him on the council bench wearing distinctive garments. Again, it is likely Paul simply didn't recognize him due to poor eyesight and believed some lesser official had ordered the indignity (Acts 22:30–23:5).[6]

---

6. In addition, it may be that Luke's presence with Paul during his travels represented practical medical assistance needed by the apostle due to his disability.

All of this evidence indicates that Paul experienced impaired eyesight after having seen the glorified Jesus on the Damascus Road. Though he attributes the thorn to the devil, for he would have viewed all infirmity and weakness as originating with him, Paul also interprets his weak eyesight as a sign of God's grace and calling to the Gentiles. Paul's spiritual insight into the eternal purposes of God for the nations increases as a result of seeing Jesus on the road even as his physical sight decreases. His spiritual sight is in inverse relationship to his physical sight. It is not farfetched to think Paul, identifying with Israel's first prophet, went to the very place where Moses' appearance was transfigured by God's glory and experienced a type of transfiguration of his own.[7]

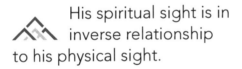

His spiritual sight is in inverse relationship to his physical sight.

Thus, Paul went to Mt. Sinai to find confirmation of God's calling to the Gentiles. He would have found there the same confirmation that Moses received on the mountain. The Book of Exodus reports that the assembly of the Israelites at Mt. Sinai in worship was a sign to

---

7. "When Moses came down from Mount Sinai, with the two tablets of the testimony in his hand ... Moses did not know that the skin of his face shone because he had been talking with God. Aaron and all the people of Israel saw Moses, and behold, the skin of his face shone, and they were afraid to come near him.... And when Moses had finished speaking with them, he put a veil over his face. Whenever Moses went in before the Lord to speak with him, he would remove the veil, until he came out.... And Moses would put the veil over his face again" (Exodus 34:29–35).

Moses of God's purpose for leading Israel out of Egypt.
It was a sign that confirmed his calling and enabled him
to go before them. However, Moses did not accomplish
this through his own ability, wisdom, or power. It was
not by good fortune or by natural events that the people
escaped Pharaoh. God's power did it. So also, Paul found
confirmation of his calling to the Gentiles at the same
Sinai. He learned there in advance that the Gentiles would
be delivered by the power of God and not by Paul's own
learning, knowledge, or talent. Writing to the Corinthians,
Paul says:

> And I, when I came to you, brothers, did not come
> proclaiming to you the testimony of God with lofty
> speech or wisdom. For I decided to know nothing
> among you except Jesus Christ and him crucified.
> And I was with you in weakness and in fear and much
> trembling, and my speech and my message were not
> in plausible words of wisdom, but in demonstration
> of the Spirit and of power, so that your faith might
> not rest in the wisdom of men but in the power of
> God (1 Corinthians 2:1–5).

The fulfillment of the sign of worship at Mt. Sinai
was a check to Moses' pride and one of the reasons he
remained humble despite the extraordinary accomplishments of his ministry. It explains what fueled his
commitment to the Israelites despite their ongoing
criticism of him. In the same way, Paul's calling on
the Damascus Road and confirmation later in Arabia
remained a check to his pride. To the Galatians, he says

that he will not exalt in his accomplishments because he knows he has not ascertained the meaning of the cross on his own but by the revelation given by God: "Far be it from me to boast except in the cross of our Lord Jesus Christ" (Galatians 6:14). Paul makes similar remarks to the Corinthians when he says that he has as much reason as any to boast in accomplishments: he is a Hebrew, an Israelite, a descendent of Abraham, and a servant of Christ (2 Corinthians 11:18). To boast of these things, however, is foolishness. Paul then reminds his readers that he has been whipped with lashes and beaten with rods. He has been stoned and left for dead, and he has even been shipwrecked. Throughout his ministry, he has lived in constant danger. After reciting all these things, Paul writes, "If I must boast, I will boast of the things that show my weakness" (2 Corinthians 11:16–30). Why these things? Why weakness? Because such things show God's power and highlight His greatness.

It is in this recitation that Paul mentions visions and revelations.

> I know a man in Christ who fourteen years ago was caught up to the third heaven—whether in the body or out of the body I do not know, God knows. And I know that this man was caught into paradise— whether in the body or out of the body I do not know, God knows—and he heard things that cannot be told, which man may not utter. On behalf of this man I will boast, but on my own behalf I will not boast (2 Corinthians 12:2–5).

Paul's mountaintop experience indelibly marked him from that moment onward. Traveling the road of his own certainty and self-assurance, Paul came face-to-face with the misdirection of his zeal. Jesus asked, "Why are you persecuting me?" (Acts 9:4). Like the unbelieving and confused generation (*genea apistos kai diestrammenē*) of Israel in the wilderness, who time after time misinterpreted God's gracious activity in their midst ("You have brought us out here to die!"), Paul was confused and misled in his understanding about Jesus and His followers.[8] The revelation God gave him not only straightened his thinking, but it also remained at the forefront of his consciousness and self-understanding and became the primary way that he understood himself throughout his life. In his letters to his followers, Paul consistently identifies himself as a "persecutor" of Jesus and His church (Galatians 1:13; Philippians 3:6). Three times Luke describes Paul's encounter with Jesus, and each time Luke highlights his persecution of Jesus and His followers (Acts 9:1–9; 22:6–11; 26:12–18). Paul does not refer to himself in this way to engage in some type of penitential verbal self-flagellation. He does not wallow in his previous ignorance and misguided zeal. Rather, he draws attention to his persecution because he knows who he was and the transformation he has experienced. This memory and the thorn that came with it keep Paul from boasting in his

---

8. Balz and Schneider, *Exegetical Dictionary of the New Testament*, vol. 1. The term for *twist* is *diastrephō*, which also means *confuse* or *go astray*. It occurs seven times in the New Testament (Matthew 17:17; Luke 9:41, 23:2; Acts 13:8, 10, 20:30; Philippians 2:15).

achievements in ministry. Like Moses, Paul does not boast except for the revelation and new sight he was given and the privilege of going to the nations.

> Like Moses, Paul does not boast except for the revelation and new sight he was given and the privilege of going to the nations.

CHRIST'S SINAI GIFT

Mt. Sinai is very much on Paul's mind when he writes to the Ephesians. Midway through the letter, he exhorts the people to "walk in a manner worthy of the calling to which you have been called." Paul says their daily life must be consistent with their calling to be sons and daughters of God (Ephesians 1:4–6), who have been fitted together as a temple for His presence (Ephesians 2:19–22). As one body, they will fulfill this purpose by manifesting the Spirit's fruit—humility, gentleness, patience, love, and peace—in unity together.[9] To be formed into one body of the Spirit is to be formed into one people of worship.[10] It is why Paul writes: "You were called to the one hope that belongs to your call—one Lord, one faith, one baptism,

---

9. Pinnock, *Flame of Love*, 21–48. The unity manifested by the church reflects the presence of the Spirit, given the fact the Spirit is the personal expression of love shared by God the Father and God the Son in their unity of relationship.
10. Pastor Jack Hayford develops the insight of the work of the Spirit in the formation of the body of Christ with the worship of God by His people in several of his books.

one God and Father of all, who is over all and through all and in all" (Ephesians 4:4–6). The hope of their calling (to be God's body or holy temple) involves the worship of all the nations.

How is the hope of God's people related to the worship of the nations? As already noted in several places, Israel was called to lead the nations in the worship of God as "a kingdom of priests and a holy nation" (Exodus 19:6). They would do this by manifesting what Paul refers to as "one Lord, one faith, one baptism, one God and Father of all, who is over all and through all and in all." This single statement encapsulates the entire Exodus story: Israel was to declare one Lord to the nations by making known to them the name God gave of Himself (Yahweh) to Moses; they were to show one faith by modeling the only way of life acceptable to Yahweh through the Torah; they were to celebrate their deliverance from death to life through the Red Sea as one baptism; and they were to testify to the nations that the God who had delivered them from Egypt was their (the nations') God too—one God and Father of all. In this passage, Paul is saying that God's desire is for all people to know Him as God (one Lord) and share in the life He gives (one faith) by being delivered from their own places of bondage through the death and resurrection of His Son (one baptism). The hope of the church's calling and the message they've been given for others represents God's desire that they participate in bringing about knowledge of Him, life with Him, and deliverance in Him through the Spirit, because He wants to do among others what He did for Israel.

According to Paul, the Ephesians' calling will be accomplished as they worship and serve Jesus who is seated at God's right hand in heaven with all things under His feet (Ephesians 1:20–22). This is possible because God has given "Christ's gift" to them. What is this gift? It is the gift of His Spirit at Pentecost. To understand this gift, Paul quotes from Psalm 68:

> When he ascended on high he led a host of
>   captives,
> and he *gave* gifts to men (Ephesians 4:8).

Paul reinterprets David's song by changing the emphasis from God's reception of gifts to His giving of gifts in order to assert that Jesus has given His Spirit to the church (Christ's gift) so that His followers will be able to live in unity and carry out their priestly responsibility of worship. They will be able to worship ("the work of ministry") with the help of Spirit-enabled apostles, prophets, evangelists, pastors, and teachers. Paul describes this work of ministry in terms of a walk of love, light, and wisdom that parallels Israel's walk in the way of Torah given by Moses. (Throughout the story of the Exodus, Israel's covenantal life lived in obedience to the commandments given at Sinai is described in terms of walking.) And Paul compares this walk to being filled with the Spirit by which they speak to one another "in psalms and hymns and spiritual songs, singing and making melody to the Lord with your heart, giving thanks always and for everything to God" (Ephesians 5:18–20). Christ's gift refers to the sending of His Spirit at Pentecost that enables followers to carry out the work of their priestly ministry in a worshipful manner.

SINAI THEOLOGY

There is no place for pride in the life of those who have been to Mt. Sinai. The vision of God experienced there, like that experienced by Paul, exposes our own lives to blinding light. The shadow that we cast is sharply outlined against the light of His glory. We see ourselves for the first time when we are confronted with the vision that God gives of Himself to us. Such a vision does not lead to despair, but results in freedom to take the good news of relationship with God and the possibility of worship in His presence to all the nations. When we experience the revelation God gives of Himself to us as He did to Israel on Mt. Sinai, our vision of Him, ourselves, and our purpose in the world is forever changed. We see with new eyes that God forgives, restores, and calls us to worship.

> There is no place for pride in the life of those who have been to Mt. Sinai.

David's Psalm 68 refers to God's presence at the temple as "Sinai in the sanctuary." Paul understands the psalm to be prophetic of the gift of the Spirit that Jesus gave to His followers at Pentecost and now has given to the Ephesians so that they might live in unity as a new people from whom the nations will experience true worship of God. In short,

Paul says that Jesus gave the Spirit so that His followers might personally experience Sinai in their own lives and be a people who live in unity and walk in His love as ancient Israel did. We are to walk as children of light in wisdom as we give continual praise to the Lord with all our hearts (Deuteronomy 6:5). We are to walk in the way given to Israel at Sinai, and we will do this with the help of Spirit-anointed leaders as we grow into the body of the Messiah.

Reflection and Discussion

1. Where does Paul go when he leaves Damascus? Why does he go there?
2. When Paul writes to the Ephesians, he refers to "Christ's gift." What is this gift, and for what purpose is it given?
3. Describe your experience with Christ's gift.

11

Peter's Recollection of Sinai: A Royal Priesthood

PETER, JAMES, AND John were with Jesus on the Mount of Transfiguration. The three disciples beheld God's glory upon Jesus and heard the heavenly voice say that He was God's beloved Son. It was an experience that was cold-pressed onto Peter's consciousness.[1] According to Matthew and Mark, the three disciples fell to the ground in awe of the glory of God upon Jesus, and from that moment on, Peter associated the glory on the mountain with Sinai. It is why he asked Jesus if he should build tabernacles or tents (*skēnas*) for all of them to stay there.[2] Peter's suggestion shows that he was recalling the way Israel lived in the wilderness during their journey to Canaan. The vision

---

1. Helyer, *The Life and Witness of Peter* 2012), 49–50. Larry Helyer remarks that the impact of the experience on the disciples was "overwhelming."
2. Ibid. Helyer believes that the transfiguration occurred on Mt. Hermon. He writes, "Peter's reference to dwellings recalls the Feast of Tabernacles (Hebrew *sukkôt*) in which observant Jews build temporary huts and live in them for a week to commemorate the wilderness wanderings and God's faithful provision both then and now (Leviticus 23:23–25, 29–43; Deuteronomy 16:13–15)."

of Moses and Elijah with Jesus on the mountain stirred Peter's imagination, leading him to suggest an activity that would reprise the original one in some way. His later letters show the lasting impression the mountain made on him.[3] In his first letter, Peter describes his readers as a "royal priesthood" (1 Peter 2:9), referring to the identity God gave to Israel at Mt. Sinai when He brought them out of Egypt. In his second letter, Peter refers to his experience with *majesty* on what he calls "the holy mountain" (2 Peter 1:18).

MAJESTY ON THE MOUNTAIN (2 PETER)

The context of both letters is important for appreciating Peter's view of Sinai. In the second letter, which resembles a sermon given in Greek rhetorical style, Peter begins by exhorting his readers to live out their calling and to make their election sure. Despite the Greek style and vocabulary, Peter grounds his underlying message in Israel's deliverance story. He tells his readers to share in "the divine nature" (2 Peter 1:4). Through God's divine power, they

---

3. Davids, *The Letters of 2 Peter and Jude*, 121–158. Most New Testament scholars doubt that Peter wrote the two letters attributed to him. They point to the literary and rhetorical style of the letters and their vocabulary, especially 2 Peter and its Greek philosophical themes, and say that Peter could not have written them. The letters may have been written by one of Peter's followers long after his death in Rome in the 60s. With respect to 2 Peter, some believe that it is an example of a pseudepigraphal testament, well known in Jewish literature then, and would not have been read as from Peter by Christians at that time. For an informative overview and discussion of the authorship of 2 Peter, as well as its genre, language, and style, see Peter H. Davids' introduction to the letter in his commentary.

have been delivered from the corruption of the world, and, for this reason, they should cultivate a virtuous life in preparation for "the eternal kingdom of our Lord and Savior Jesus Christ" by living according to His promises (2 Peter 1:11). This exhortation sounds familiar because it recalls the story of the Exodus when God delivered the Israelites from the corruption of Egypt to become His sons and daughters through the manifestation of His great power in the plagues, the Red Sea, the manna, and the commandments He gave them at Mt. Sinai.

Moses said that the people of Israel would affirm their election by living in fidelity with God through the covenant. In the same way, Peter says his readers can make their "calling and election" sure by cultivating the qualities of faith, virtue, knowledge, self-control, steadfastness, godliness, brotherly affection, and love (2 Peter 1:5–11). He is thinking of the covenant in a new way related to the Spirit and says he will remind them of these things, for these attributes are signs of God's nature and presence in their own lives. This is not any different from the exhortation given by God to the Israelites to share in His nature: "Be holy as I am holy" (Leviticus 11:45, 19:2, 20:26). The Israelites were to share God's holiness because He had delivered them in His great power and given them His words.

Peter's readers can be assured of their election, moreover, because the teaching they have received from him is not based on "cleverly devised myths" but on eyewitness testimony of the "power and coming of [the] Lord Jesus Christ" (1:16), which he describes as "God's majesty." What he means is that the teaching he gives is not just any old story but is related to the revelation he received on the mountain with Jesus. Specifically, Peter recalls the transfiguration of Jesus on the mountain where he heard the voice from heaven speak:

> We were eyewitnesses of his majesty. For when he received honor and glory from God the Father, and the voice was borne to him by the Majestic Glory, **"This is my beloved Son, with whom I am well pleased**," we ourselves heard this very voice borne from heaven, for we were with him on the holy mountain (2 Peter 1:16–18).

Peter was there at Mt. Sinai, where God spoke His Word and manifested His glory. He wasn't there with Moses at the time of the Exodus, of course, but he was there with Jesus and saw the majesty of God envelop Him in the presence of Moses and Elijah.

What Peter preaches is not groundless myth but rather the grounded truth of his personal experience with Jesus, including his experience with Jesus on Sinai. It issues from the Word that God spoke on the mountain: "This is my beloved Son, with whom I am well pleased." It is *this* Word that Peter has made known to his readers: Jesus is God's Son who enjoys His favor and blessing. He says that it is prophetic and "more sure" (*bebaios*) than clever stories because its origin rests with God and not with man. In fact, it is the very same prophetic word that God revealed to Peter at Caesarea Philippi, which Jesus said was divine revelation.

It is prophetic in the same way that Jesus' Sermon on the Mount is prophetic. At the end of that sermon, Jesus exhorted Peter and the disciples to live their lives on the words He had just given to them. If they do, they will be like a man who builds his house on the rock; it will stand despite the storms that come against it. Sometime later, after Peter confesses Jesus to be the Son of God, Jesus rejoices because for the first time someone other than Himself has received knowledge of His identity as God's Son. Jesus is so excited that He pronounces Peter "blessed." The disciple has received a revelation from the Father: "Flesh and blood has not revealed this to you, but my Father who is in heaven" (Matthew 16:17). Jesus then says that upon "this rock" He will build His church. What is the rock? Though many think the rock is Peter, it is better to think of the rock as the revelatory word Peter has spoken through the grace of God the Father. It is the rock in the same way that Jesus' Sermon on the Mount is a rock for His disciples. But this is not all. It is a rock in the same way God's law at Sinai was the rock that Israel was to live by when God revealed it to Moses by His Spirit on the mountain. "Upon this rock" means upon the Sinai words of revelation that God speaks. When God's people live by the revelatory word given by His Spirit, Jesus says His church will be established and not even the power of hell will be able to overthrow it (Matthew 16:18). What Peter means when he says that his message is more sure than human myths is that God's Sinai word is greater than the wildest and most imaginative stories that people can tell. It is greater than all the stories of gods and goddesses that the nations told one another then or have told at any other time.[4] Peter says it is prophetic and is like "a lamp shining in a dark place" (2 Peter 1:9). It is like the Word of God in fire on Sinai in a dark wilderness. And just as the commandments were not merely Moses' words, so also Peter's teaching isn't simply his own interpretation of things. It represents God's will expressed through His Holy Spirit (2 Peter 1:19–21).

> What is the rock? Though many think the rock is Peter, it is better to think of the rock as the revelatory word Peter has spoken through the grace of God the Father. "Upon this rock" means upon the Sinai words of revelation that God speaks.

A KINGDOM OF PRIESTS (1 PETER)

Peter recalls the gift of the Spirit on the Day of Pentecost and shows his understanding of its Sinai meaning when he calls his followers "a royal priesthood, a holy nation" (1 Peter 2:9). He was with Jesus at the ascension and heard Him say, "I am sending the promise of my Father upon you. But stay in the city until you are clothed with power from on high" (Luke 24:49). And Peter was with the disciples on

---

4. For background on the Hellenistic context of 1–2 Peter, see Witherington, *Letters and Homilies for Hellenized Christians*.

the Day of Pentecost when the Spirit came upon them in fire (Acts 2). Those events shaped his understanding of his calling and ministry.

Several features of Peter's first letter indicate that he is thinking of the Exodus and Sinai as he writes. For one thing, he refers to his readers as an exilic or exodus people (1 Peter 1:1). They are to "fear" the Lord throughout the time of their exile (1 Peter 1:17) and resist the urges of the flesh while in exile (1 Peter 2:11). This kind of identification would have caused his readers to see themselves not only in relation to the people of the Assyrian and Babylonian exiles but also to the generation of the Exodus. Those later exilic events were regarded at the time they occurred as a second Exodus experience. And the fact that Peter says they are "elect" would certainly have caused them to remember the Exodus story where the Israelites are described as the elect of God: "For you are a people holy to the Lord your God. The Lord your God has chosen (*eklektos* in the Septuagint) you to be a people for his treasured possession" (Deuteronomy 7:6).

Peter exhorts his readers to keep hope and maintain holiness in their lives despite hardship and suffering (1 Peter 2:19–24). They are not to grumble as the Israelites did in the wilderness when they experienced hardship and suffered lack of food and water. Instead, they should show hospitality to one another (1 Peter 4:9).

Finally, and most importantly, Peter says that his people are:

a royal priesthood, a holy nation, a people for his own possession, that you may proclaim the excellencies of him who called you out of darkness into his marvelous light.... Once you had not received mercy, but now you have received mercy (1 Peter 2:9–10).

Here, Peter recalls Pentecost, since on that day God gave His Spirit to Jesus' disciples so they could serve as His ministers and be His priesthood to the nations. Pentecost not only redefined Peter's understanding of himself and his vocation, but it shaped his understanding of all disciples. He says that they are people of mercy, joining them to the Israelites, the original people of God's mercy, having received His mercy in the wilderness: "For you are a people holy to the Lord your God.... Know therefore that the Lord your God is God, the faithful God who keeps covenant and steadfast love (*hesed*) with those who love him" (Deuteronomy 7:6, 9). Through their good works, Peter's followers are to give the Gentiles reason to glorify God. As priests, they enable the nations to worship God through the fulfillment of their priestly duties, which Peter describes as honorable conduct (1 Peter 2:12).

Prior to this declaration Peter says the people are to be living stones, related to the one living stone (Jesus) who was rejected, to be built up into a spiritual house and "a holy priesthood" (1 Peter 2:4–5), recalling Paul's description of the followers of Jesus being formed into a holy people by the Spirit in his letter to the Ephesians:

"You are fellow citizens with the saints and members of the household of God, built on the foundation of the apostles and prophets, Christ Jesus himself being the cornerstone, in whom the whole structure, being joined together, grows into a holy temple in the Lord. In him you also are being built together into a dwelling place for God by the Spirit" (Ephesians 2:19–22).

Peter then quotes a couple of Old Testament passages that describe a discarded cornerstone upon which the spiritual house is built and says the honor to be a part of the house is reserved for those who believe and not those who "disobey the word" (1 Peter 2:6–8). This expression is a clear reference to the Exodus generation who disobeyed God's Word of promise that He would lead them into a land of milk and honey. They grumbled and accused Him of leading them into the wilderness to kill them. In their uncertainty and fear, the people lost sight of the signs God had given and could not believe. Instead, they looked upon the lack of water and food, the presence of giants in the land, and the magnitude of God's call upon their lives. Peter tells his Jewish readers not to be like the Exodus generation but rather to believe the words he is writing to them.

At this point, Peter quotes Isaiah ("A stone of stumbling, and a rock of offense") and shows he is thinking of the Exodus story and Pentecost. The passage of the quote (Isaiah 8:1–9:7) describes the days prior to the Assyrian exile when the prophet calls to Judah and urges the king not to join a coalition being formed by Syria and Israel against Assyria despite the political wisdom of such a move: "Because this people ... rejoice

over Rezin and the son of Remaliah (Syria and Israel) ...
the Lord is bringing up against them the waters of the
River, mighty and many, the king of Assyria and all his
glory" (Isaiah 8:5–7). Isaiah urges the people to trust in
God despite the dire circumstances "and he will become a
sanctuary and a stone of offense and a rock of stumbling
to both houses of Israel" (Isaiah 8:14). For those who
trust Him and believe His word, God will be a refuge, but
for those who place their trust in the coalition, He will be
a stumbling rock. For his part, Isaiah is determined "to
bind up the testimony and seal the teaching" of God's
word concerning this situation (Isaiah 8:16). Those who
don't will pass through the land in distress and hunger,
and they will "speak contemptuously against their king
and their God" and be in darkness (Isaiah 8:21–22). They
will experience exactly what the Israelites did in the
wilderness when they were hungry, became enraged, and
spoke against Moses and God: "You have brought us out
into this wilderness to kill this whole assembly!"
(Exodus 16:3). There is hope, however, for those who
anguish over this as God will make "glorious the way of
the sea" (Isaiah 9:1). Isaiah then declares: "The people
who walked in darkness have seen a great light; those who
dwelt in a land of deep darkness, on them light has shone"
(Isaiah 9:2). Just as God brought Israel out from the land
of darkness in Egypt by the great light from the fire at the
tabernacle (Exodus 40:38), so also Isaiah foresees a
similar deliverance for God's people at a future time.
God's deliverance will conclude with the birth of a son
who will lead the government with wisdom and might,

justice and righteousness, in fulfillment of the promise made to David.

> For those who trust Him and believe His word, God will be a refuge, but for those who place their trust in the coalition, He will be a stumbling rock.

For to us a child is born, to us a son is given; and the government shall be upon his shoulder, and his name shall be called Wonderful Counselor, Mighty God, Everlasting Father, Prince of Peace. Of the increase of his government and of peace there will be no end, on the throne of David and over his kingdom, to establish it and to uphold it with justice and with righteousness from this time forth and forevermore (Isaiah 9:6–7).

This passage in Isaiah and all its allusions to the Exodus describe the situation of Peter's Jewish readers. They were facing difficult circumstances like the people at the time of Isaiah and earlier in the time of Moses, but they must choose to believe the Sinai-words that God had spoken and is continuing to speak through Peter himself. They must remember that they are a royal priesthood, in the same way Israel was a kingdom of priests, and they are to live as such despite the suffering and hardships they will endure. They will be able to do this through the help of the Spirit who has moved upon them and has in effect moved the mountain of Sinai into their very midst.

SINAI THEOLOGY

Peter teaches us that Sinai is the place of God's majesty where He speaks words of revelation to His people. It is there that they hear words greater than all other words that governors, princes, and kings have ever spoken or will ever speak: "This is my beloved Son with whom I am well pleased." Not only is Sinai the place where God makes known His words to His people, but it is also the place where His people speak prophetically to the world. We proclaim the majesty of our God as a royal priesthood who has received His mercy and been given the privilege of doing good works—even in difficult circumstances—just as that first Sinai generation was called to do. Such good works in response to God's majesty and mercy are the essence of Sinai worship.

Reflection and Discussion

1. When was Peter on Mt. Sinai?
2. What does Peter mean when he writes that his word is "more sure" than myths and stories?
3. Do you find it hard to do good works when you find yourself in difficult circumstances? What would Peter say?

12

A Higher Sinai

SACRIFICIAL WORSHIP

The author of Hebrews does not look backward in the
direction of Mt. Sinai. He does not look to the mountain of
Moses and Elijah. In his mind, that wilderness mountain is
a foothill of the one that rises in heaven. He looks forward
and upward to "Mount Zion and to the city of the living
God, the heavenly Jerusalem" (Hebrews 12:22) and urges
his readers to look in that direction too, for it is there
that they will one day meet angels, the gathering of the
firstborn, and God Himself. It is there they will meet Jesus.
Mt. Zion is higher than Mt. Sinai in the same way that
Jesus is greater than Moses and His sacrifice greater than
all the sacrifices of the tabernacle and the temple. If God
spoke with authority from Mt. Sinai, how much more is
the authority with which He speaks through Jesus in Zion
and how much more imperative to act upon His words and
worship Him?

> See that you do not refuse him who is speaking. For
> if they did not escape when they refused him who
> warned them on earth, much less will we escape if we

reject him who warns from heaven. At that time his voice shook the earth, but now he has promised, "Yet once more I will shake not only the earth but also the heavens" (Hebrews 12:25–26).

For this reason, "let us offer to God acceptable worship, with reverence and awe, for our God is a consuming fire" (Hebrews 12:28–29).

The author may not view Sinai being as high as Zion, but he recognizes that at Sinai God spoke His word and the earth shook in anticipation of the worship of God. This leads him to exhort his readers to acceptable or pleasing worship in reverence. The word for worship used here is *latreuō*, which occurs throughout the Septuagint to describe the sacrificial worship offered at the temple. The type of worship required by Sinai as well as Zion, according to Hebrews, is sacrificial. It involves endurance (the theme of the preceding chapters) and desire. Not all the Israelites escaped the wilderness because not all of them were able to endure. Their desire for their past life was greater than their desire for God's future promise. The sacrifice that is pleasing to God is that which is made of a person's heart or desire. As said previously, to ascend the mountain is to risk being transformed in the presence of God through worship. Pleasing worship at the mountain trusts the word that God speaks and acts upon that word with heart despite what circumstances may show.

> The sacrifice that is pleasing to God is that which is made of a person's heart or desire.

For the author of Hebrews, Mt. Zion is the eternal expression of Mt. Sinai. It is the heavenly mountain that is the archetype of the earthly one. In his mind, the fire-filled words of Sinai are amplified multiple times on Mt. Zion, shaking not only the foundations of the earth but also the pillars of all creation. This word is spoken by God, a consuming fire whose presence eternally alters those who come to Him. He is the God who invites us to enter His fire and forever be purified and so transformed that we will not even recognize ourselves. He wants to change us to look like Him and to reflect His nature: "Let us make man in our image, after our likeness" (Genesis 1:26).

THE GLORY OF THE NATIONS

The Book of Revelation concludes with John the Visionary standing on "a great high mountain" seeing the descent of the city of Jerusalem from heaven in glory (Revelation 21:10). The gates and foundations of the city he sees represent the people of Israel and the apostles who are engulfed in the glory of God, which is a light to the nations: "By [the city's] light will the nations walk, and the kings of the earth will bring their glory into it.... They will bring into it the glory and the honor of the nations" (Revelation 21:23–26). Through this city flows a river with trees of life on either bank, the leaves of which are for "the healing of the nations" (Revelation 22:1–2). John sees the people of God filled with the life and Spirit of God, refreshing and restoring all others to wholeness.

There on the mountain, John sees God's glory in Israel and the glory of the nations. He sees what God intended when He first appeared at Sinai, spoke His word to Israel, and called the people to His priesthood. John sees that God has always intended for His glory to be in the midst of His people—for His light to shine through them as a city on a hill as they live by His words. In this way, all people everywhere might see His glory and add their own devotion by walking in a similar way. When John says that the nations will walk in the glory of God, he means that they will live by the example that Israel provides through her own devotion to the words of the covenant. The glory that shone from Moses' face as he received the words of the covenant was the glory that all of Israel was to show by living according to those same words. Through the apostles who had received the words of Jesus, God's glory will be reflected to all people.

John sees that as these people (the nations) come into the New Jerusalem, they will be healed (*therapeuō*). He sees that they will be restored to a place of relationship with God and thereby restored to the purpose of that relationship, which is worship: "No longer will there be anything accursed, but the throne of God and of the Lamb will be in it, and his servants will worship him.... And they will reign forever and ever" (Revelation 22:3–5). The nations will be joined to Israel and together become the servant who worships God and as a result will rule over all creation. The word worship (*latreuō*), as noted above, describes sacrificial temple offerings. To sacrifice means to give what is vital or necessary. Nothing less than the complete devotion of one's life is the pleasing sacrifice that God accepts, and it is this that the nations and Israel will give to God in response to the pleasing sacrifice of His Son. God's glory in Israel will include the glory of the nations as they are restored to worship by God and His Lamb.

> Nothing less than the complete devotion of one's life is the pleasing sacrifice that God accepts, and it is this that the nations and Israel will give to God in response to the pleasing sacrifice of His Son.

SINAI THEOLOGY

The worship of Sinai that God desires from His people is sacrificial in nature. It is worship that endures through trials and hardship and flows out of a desire for relationship with Him that is greater than all other desires. When we are willing to risk the reward of worship by persevering by faith in the word that God speaks in such times, He is present to us and we are changed by it.

Sinai encourages us to look forward with hope and optimism because Sinai is ultimately where we see what covenantal relationship with God looks like. It is where we see what our vocation and mission in life involve. And it is where we see that the essence of life is understanding each other, living in unity, and having love for one another as we worship God together.

Reflection and Discussion

1. What type of worship does the writer of Hebrews expect God's people to offer Him? What does this type of worship look like in your own life?
2. What is the result of hearing and responding to God's word from Mt. Zion?
3. How does John's vision from a "great high mountain" recall Mt. Sinai?

Conclusion

WHEN GOD DESCENDED upon Mt. Sinai in the fire of His personal presence, speaking in the thunderous voice of the nations, the people of Israel drew back in fear and sent Moses ahead to hear His words. They were shaken by the force of His coming and unprepared for the power by which He intended to purify them. They were startled by the new vocation of sonship He had delivered them out of Egypt to experience. They were to be sons and daughters with God as their Father. They were overwhelmed by the mission God had planned for them. They were to know Him so closely that they could lead the nations in His adoration. God had brought His people to the mountain to mold them into a holy people who would welcome His word and manifest His wisdom in their lives. He gathered them in the wilderness to shape them into a kingdom of priests who would give the whole world an example of worship.

Beginning with the story of the Exodus and concluding with John's revelation of Jesus, Scripture reveals Mt. Sinai to be the high place where God speaks His word and reveals His ways. It is the place where His wisdom is made known and His people discover who He is. It is the instruction on how they are to live securely before Him and generously with one another. And it is the sacred place where His people are purified so that they may offer pleasing worship to Him and persuasive testimony to the nations of His goodness. To climb up into such a place requires faith. It requires an obedient response to the word that God speaks and a willingness to think and act in a new way based on what He has already done. It requires trust in God's promises despite the cares of everyday life or the crises that threaten the very foundations of life.

We learn from the stories of Sinai that to climb to the top of the mountain is to hear God's voice. It is to hear the word He speaks in thunder and the word He speaks in silence. It is to hear God's words in our hearts, to feel His words in our bones, and to have His words on our lips.

Like Moses, whose face radiated with the brilliance of God's word, and like Jesus, whose entire being shone like the sun because he lived in the power of the Spirit and "It is written," those who climb Sinai are changed by that same word. They are given new garments to lead people in the worship of God by showing the way of forgiveness. They are a royal priesthood, clothed with His Spirit, for the high privilege of bringing reconciliation to the world.

This means that to climb to the top of the mountain is to see God, His way, and His world with new eyes. Like Paul, who looked upon the glorified Jesus on the road to Damascus and saw God's purposes in a revolutionary light, *our vision is transfigured* when we see that God redeems what people count as lost and purifies what people claim to be cursed in His ambition to bring about a unified worship in Israel and in the world.

Few if any of us will ever climb the physical Mt. Sinai as did Moses, Elijah, or Paul. Few of us will ever hear His voice in fire, thunder, and silence as they did. Yet, it is God's desire for every one of us to experience the Sinai of His word and the transforming power of His worship. We must never forget that worship is not just for God's pleasure, but according to Pastor Jack Hayford, it is designed for our benefit.[1] Worship changes us. By giving His Spirit at Pentecost to those who waited for the promise of the Father by faith, God was planting the mountain of revelation in a new temple, not one made of mortar and stone but with living stones of flesh and blood. This remains God's desire: that the mountain be planted in all people and that all would experience Sinai in the sanctuary where the Spirit of God is present to speak revelatory words of life, inspire grateful worship, and transfigure people into a holy priesthood, who offer God's forgiveness and proclaim His goodness to a world waiting to be led in worship.

---

1. Hayford, *The Reward of Worship*, 45–46.

Appendix 1

The Spiral of the Spirit

THE EARLY CHURCH appreciated the relationship between Easter and Pentecost and saw the two celebrations as the beginning and concluding events of one holy season.[1] It was a season that correlated with the two primary events of the Exodus: the deliverance through the Red Sea and the giving of the law at Mt. Sinai. For this reason, Christians performed catechisms and baptisms of new believers during this time. They were reenacting the important events of the Exodus when Israel was baptized in the Red Sea and given the Torah at Sinai. In their mind, the Spirit who was at work then to give new life was also present now to give new life and what was needed to live it. This twofold work of the Spirit is depicted in the following diagram, which is loosely based on the double helix DNA model developed by James Watson and Francis Crick in the 1950s. DNA strands are separate but parallel and connected, and they provide the information needed by cells to perform various functions.[2] In a similar

---

1. Skarsaune, *In the Shadow of the Temple*, 389.
2. Meyer, *Signature in the Cell*, 58–84.

way, the Spirit works in the lives of men and women to know God's word so they may participate with Him in the world He has created.

THE SPIRAL OF THE SPIRIT

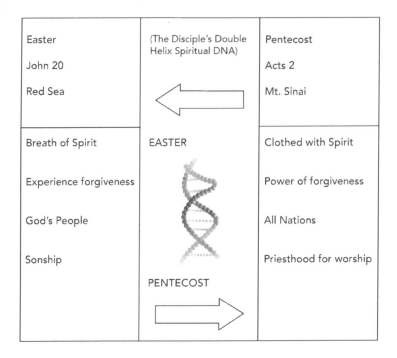

Easter	(The Disciple's Double Helix Spiritual DNA)	Pentecost
John 20		Acts 2
Red Sea		Mt. Sinai
Breath of Spirit	EASTER	Clothed with Spirit
Experience forgiveness		Power of forgiveness
God's People		All Nations
Sonship		Priesthood for worship
	PENTECOST	

This representation shows that the work of the Spirit in conversion moves us into a new relationship with God and His people. This is described in the Gospels as "the kingdom of God." It is here that we begin to worship God. This does not represent the totality of the Spirit's work, however. The same Spirit compels us back into the world after the manner of Jesus as we become conscious of our priestly calling and responsibilities in worship. The Spirit gives us authority to live out this calling and fulfill the great commission. The primary responsibility is to lead others into the life of worship that we have begun. This movement into the kingdom and into the world may be called the *Spiral of the Spirit* in that the ministry of the Spirit first draws us out of the world into a worshipful relationship with God and His people and then compels us to move back into the world for the priestly purpose of reconciling the world in the worship of God we've been given.

The story of the Exodus shows this kind of movement. At the outset, God identifies the Hebrew people as His "son" (Exodus 4:23; Hosea 11:1). The Israelites belong to God, even though they have not yet received the law at Mt. Sinai. God gives His name to them, leads them through the Red Sea, and feeds them with manna because they are His son. It is at this time that the son ceases being like the Egyptians and begins to learn who his Father is and the nature of his calling. This reaches a climax at Mt. Sinai, where God gives His law to the son so he may serve Him and lead the nations in worship. The son will do this once he has entered Canaan and begun to live by the word God has given to him. The light of the glory of that word as it shines in his life will be an example to the nations of the presence of God in their midst.

Appendix 2

Mt. Sinai and Pentecost

A COMPARISON OF the giving of the law at Mt. Sinai with the giving of the Spirit on the day of Pentecost reveals several common features and suggests a shared theological understanding of these two events.

Exodus	Story Features	Acts 1–2	Story Features
19:3–6	God promises that the people will be His "treasured possession," a "kingdom of priests," and a "holy nation."	1:4–8	Jesus promises the disciples that they will receive the Holy Spirit.
19:12–24	The people wait at the base of the mountain; they are not to ascend without God's permission.	1:4	The disciples wait in Jerusalem.

Exodus	Story Features	Acts 1–2	Story Features
19:16, 19	God's presence is announced by a "loud trumpet blast" and with a loud voice (Deuteronomy 5:22).	2:2	The Spirit comes "like a mighty rushing wind."
19:18 20:18	God's presence comes in the form of smoke and fire. God speaks His word out of the fire (Deuteronomy 5:4, 22, 24, 26).	2:3	The Spirit comes in the form of "tongues of fire."
19:6	The whole earth belongs to God, and Israel will be a kingdom of priests.	2:5–11	God-fearing Jews of all nations hear the praises of God in their own languages.
20:1–17 Deuteronomy 5:6–21, 32–33	God gives Israel His words. The people are exhorted to keep God's commands as a witness to the nations.	2:14–39	Peter proclaims the gospel to the people gathered in Jerusalem. The gospel will continue to be preached until it is pronounced by Paul in Rome.

This comparison shows that the disciples would have readily interpreted their experience and celebration of Pentecost with the giving of the law at Sinai. The fact that the loud and fiery manifestation of the Spirit occurred on the day when the Jewish people celebrated the commandments given in thunder and fire would have been viewed by them as prophetic. Moreover, the question asked by God-fearing Jews who saw these things— "What does this mean?"— reflects an appreciation on their part for the prophetic nature of the display and demonstration of God's presence. The people who saw the fire and heard the praises given to God would have thought of Mt. Sinai and wondered what God was reprising in their midst. Some like the disciples would have perceived that God was giving His Spirit to them as a testimony to all people in fulfillment of His promise long ago to make Israel a kingdom of priests to the nations.

Bibliography

Balz, Horst, and Gerhard Schneider, eds. *Exegetical Dictionary of the New Testament.* Vol 1. Grand Rapids: Eerdmans, 1990.

Berger, Klaus. *Jesus and the Dead Sea Scrolls: The Truth under Lock and Key?* Translated by James S. Currie. Westminster John Knox Press, 1995.

Bockmuehl, Klaus. *Listening to the God Who Speaks: Reflections on God's Guidance from Scripture and the Lives of God's People.* Colorado Springs: Helmers & Howard, 1990.

Boersma, Hans. *Violence, Hospitality, and the Cross: Reappropriating the Atonement Tradition.* Grand Rapids, MI: Baker Academic, 2004.

Brown, Colin. Systematic Theology lectures. Fuller Theological Seminary, Pasadena, California, 1993–1997.

Coats, George W. *Moses: Heroic Man, Man of God.* Sheffield: JSOT Press, 1988.

Davids, Peter H. *The Letters of 2 Peter and Jude.* The Pillar New Testament Commentary. Grand Rapids, MI: Eerdmans, 2006.

Dumbrell, William J. *The Faith of Israel: A Theological Survey of the Old Testament.* 2nd ed. Grand Rapids, MI: Baker Academic, 2002.

Eerdman's Dictionary of the Bible. Edited by David Noel Freedman. Grand Rapids, MI: Eerdmans, 2000.

Hamilton, Victor P. *Handbook on the Historical Books.* Grand Rapids, MI: Baker Academic, 2001.

Hayford, Jack. *Glory on Your House: Welcoming God's Radiant Presence in Your Home and Church.* Grand Rapids, MI: Chosen Books, 1982.

_____. *Worship His Majesty: How Praising the King of Kings Will Change Your Life.* Ventura: Regal, 2000.

_____. *The Reward of Worship: The Joy of Fellowship with a Personal God.* Grand Rapids, MI: Chosen Books, 2005.

Hays, Richard B. *The Conversion of the Imagination: Paul as Interpreter of Israel's Scripture.* Grand Rapids, MI: Eerdmans, 2005.

Helyer, Larry R. *The Life and Witness of Peter.* Downers Grove, IL: IVP Academic, 2012.

Hoerth, Alfred J., Gerald L. Mattingly, and Edwin M. Yamauchi, eds. *Peoples of the Old Testament World.* Grand Rapids, MI: Baker Books, 1998.

Hoffmeier, James K. *Israel in Egypt: The Evidence for the Authenticity of the Exodus Tradition.* New York: Oxford University Press, 1996.

Hort, Greta, "The Plagues of Egypt." *Zeitschrift für die alttestamentliche Wissenschaft* 69 (1957): 84–103; 70 (1958): 48–59.

Huntzinger, Jon. *The Trees Will Clap Their Hands: A Garden Theology.* Bloomington: Westbow Press, 2012.

Kaiser, Walter C., Jr. *Mission in the Old Testament: Israel as a Light to the Nations.* Grand Rapids, MI: Baker Books, 2000.

Knowles, Michael P. *The Unfolding Mystery of the Divine Name: The God of Sinai in Our Midst.* Downers Grove, IL: IVP Academic, 2012.

Krakauer, Jon. *Into Thin Air: A Personal Account of the Mt. Everest Disaster.* New York: Anchor Books, 1999.

Lawrence, Paul, et. al. *The IVP Atlas of Bible History.* Downers Grove, IL: IVP Academic, 2006.

Lewis, C. S. *The Weight of Glory and Other Addresses.* San Francisco: HarperSanFrancisco, 2001.

Longman, Tremper, III. *An Introduction to the Old Testament.* 2nd ed. Grand Rapids, MI: Zondervan, 2006.

_____. "The Divine Warrior: The New Testament Use of an Old Testament Motif." *Westminster Theological Journal* 44 (Fall 1982): 290–307.

Longman, Tremper, III, and Daniel Reid. *God Is a Warrior: Studies in Old Testament Biblical Theology.* Grand Rapids, MI: Zondervan, 1995.

Meyer, Stephen C. *Signature in the Cell: DNA and the Evidence for Intelligent Design.* New York: HarperOne, 2009.

Nielsen, Kirsten. *There Is Hope for a Tree: The Tree as Metaphor in Isaiah.* Sheffield: JSOT Press, 1985.

Otto, Rudolph. *The Idea of the Holy: An Inquiry into the Non-Rational Factor in the Idea of the Divine and Its Relation to the Rational.* 2nd ed. Translated by John W. Harvey. Oxford: Oxford University Press, 1958.

Pinnock, Clark H. *Flame of Love: A Theology of the Holy Spirit.* Downers Grove, IL: IVP, 1996.

Ryken, Leland, James C. Wilhoit, and Tremper Longman, III, eds. *Dictionary of Biblical Imagery.* Downers Grove, IL: IVP, 1998.

Safrai, S., and M. Stern, with David Flusser and W.C. van Unnik. *The Jewish People in the First Century: Historical Geography, Political History, Social, Cultural, and Religious Life and Institutions.* Vol. 2. Philadelphia: Fortress Press, 1976.

Sailhamer, John H. *The Pentateuch as Narrative: A Biblical Theological Commentary.* Library of Biblical Interpretation. Grand Rapids, MI: Zondervan, 1992.

Shanks, Hershel. "Where Is Mount Sinai? The Case for Har Karkom and the Case for Saudi Arabia." *Biblical Archaeology Review 40* (March/April 2014): 30–41.

Skarsaune, Oskar. *In the Shadow of the Temple: Jewish Influences on Early Christianity.* Downers Grove: IVP Academic, 2002.

Terrien, Samuel. *The Elusive Presence: Toward a New Biblical Theology.* New York: Harper & Row, 1978.

The Complete Dead Sea Scrolls in English, Revised ed. Translated and edited with an Introduction by Geza Vermes. London: Penguin Books, 2004.

United Bible Societies. *Fauna and Flora of the Bible: Helps for Translators.* 2nd ed. New York: 1980.

Wenham, Gordon J. *Story as Torah: Reading Old Testament Narrative Ethically.* Grand Rapids, MI: Baker Academic, 2002.

Witherington, Ben III. *Letters and Homilies for Hellenized Christians, Volume II: A Socio-Rhetorical Commentary on 1–2 Peter.* Downers Grove, IL: IVP Academic, 2007.

Wright, N.T. *Paul for Everyone: Galatians and Thessalonians.* Louisville: Westminster John Knox Press, 2004. Kindle edition.

_____. "Paul, Arabia, and Elijah (Galatians 1:17)." *Journal of Biblical Literature* 115 (1996): 683–92.

_____. *The New Testament and the People of God.* Christian Origins and the Question of God. Vol. 1. Minneapolis: Fortress Press, 1992.

Scripture Index